Teaching Thinking Skills:
English/
Language Arts

Beau Fly Jones
Margaret B. Tinzmann
Lawrence B. Friedman
Beverly Butler Walker

Produced in cooperation with
the NEA Mastery In Learning Project

nea PROFESSIONAL LIBRARY
National Education Association
Washington, D.C.

Note

The opinions expressed in this publication should not be construed as representing the policy or position of the National Education Association. Materials published as part of the Building Students' Thinking Skills series are intended to be discussion documents for teachers who are concerned with specialized interests of the profession.

Library of Congress Cataloging in Publication Data

Teaching thinking skills.

   (Building students' thinking skills)
   "Produced in cooperation with the NEA Mastery in
Learning Project."
   Bibliography: p.
   1. Thought and thinking—Study and teaching.
2. English language—Study, and teaching—United
States.   3. Language arts—United States.   I. Jones,
Beau Fly.   II. Series.
LB1590.3.T48 1987   428'.007   86–21809
ISBN 0–8106–0204–0

CONTENTS

Acknowledgments 5

Introduction 7

Part 1 Learning and Instruction

Chapter 1 *The Language Arts as Thinking Processes* 12

The "New" Definition of Reading 12
Parallel Concepts in Writing 16
Parallel Concepts in Listening and Speaking 18
Parallels Among Reading, Writing, Listening
    and Speaking 20
Implications for Instruction 20
Planning Guide 1: Thinking Processes in the Language Arts 23

Chapter 2 *The Importance of Organizational Patterns* 24

Organizational Patterns in Written, Spoken, and Graphic Texts .. 24
Frames and Graphic Outlines for Organizing Thinking 28
Planning Guide 2: Frames for Generic Organizational Patterns .. 33

Chapter 3 *Strategic Teaching and Cognitive Instruction* 38

The Role of the Teacher in Cognitive Instruction 39
Specific Instructional Strategies 41
Approaches That Promote Strategic Teaching 44
Key Concepts in Cognitive Instruction and Strategic Teaching ... 46
Planning Guide 3: Thinking Processes and
    Instructional Strategies in the Language Arts 51

Part 2 *Instructional Strategies*

Chapter 4 *Content Objectives* 57

    Overview 57
    Content Example 1: Literature: Short Story or Novel 60
    Content Example 2: Content Area Passage/Rocks 65
    Content Example 3: Literature/Poetry 70

Chapter 5 *Skills Objectives* 76

    Overview 76
    Skills Example 1: Finding the Main Idea 81
    Skills Example 2: Argumentation 88

Glossary 94

Bibliography 97

ACKNOWLEDGMENTS

The framework presented in this book has evolved over a period of several years. The initial concept was developed in 1984 by Beau Jones, Lawrence Friedman, Margaret Tinzmann, and Beverly Cox in a Technical Report for the U. S. Army Research Institute for the Behavioral and Social Sciences, entitled *Content-Driven Comprehension Instruction: A Model for Army Training Literature** (61; see also 56).**

This model was subsequently revised by Annemarie Palincsar, Donna Ogle, Beau Jones, and Eileen Carr for an instructional manual entitled *Teaching Reading as Thinking* (Facilitator's Manual) published by the Association for Supervision and Curriculum Development (82). We wish to acknowledge our use of this model and thank Palincsar, Ogle, and Carr, who read portions of this manuscript.

We must also express our appreciation of the following people for their helpful comments: Jean Cameron, Principal, Carl Sandburg Junior High School, Elmhurst, Illinois; Doris Cook, Reading Education, Wisconsin Department of Public Instruction; Margaret Dunlap, teacher, Kenwood Elementary School, Cedar Rapids, Iowa; Lolita Green, Language Arts/High School Coordinator, Chicago Public Schools; Rance Howe, English/Language Arts Consultant, Anoka Hennepin, Minnesota; Mae McCarthy, English/Language Arts, California State Department of Education; Charles Suhor, Deputy Executive Director, National Council of Teachers of English; and Elaine Weber, Reading, Michigan State Department of Education. Thanks also are due to James Davis, President, JVL Systems, Evanston, Illinois, for all his help.

*Contract No. MDA–903–82–C–069. The views, opinions, and findings in this document are those of the authors and should not be construed as an official Department of the Army position, policy or decision.
**Numbers in parentheses appearing in the text refer to the Bibliography beginning on page 97.

The Authors

Beau Fly Jones is the Senior Associate for the Program on Instructional Quality and Equality at the North Central Regional Educational Laboratory, Elmhurst, Illinois. She has also coordinated several large-scale curriculum development projects in reading, writing, social studies, and vocabulary instruction for the Chicago Public Schools.

Margaret B. Tinzmann is an Instructor in the Department of Curriculum and Instruction at the National College of Education, Evanston, Illinois. She is a former special education teacher and curriculum specialist.

Lawrence B. Friedman is a Research Assistant for the Program in Instructional Quality and Equality at the North Central Regional Educational Laboratory, Elmhurst, Illinois. He has worked on curriculum development for the Chicago Public Schools and conducted independent research on comprehension and composition.

Beverly Butler Walker is an Editor for Ligature, Inc. A former elementary school teacher and college teacher, she has also worked on program development for Headstart and curriculum development for the Chicago Public Schools.

The Advisory Panel

Ann DeVenezia, English teacher, Parsippany High School, New Jersey

Vincent N. Holcomb, eighth grade teacher, Patterson Junior High School, Louisiana

Jeff Golub, English and Speech teacher, Shorecrest High School, Seattle, Washington

Barbara Johnson, English teacher, Russellville High School, Arkansas

Connie A. Lucio, English/Leadership teacher, Hillside Junior High School, Simi Valley, California

Thinking Skills Series Editors

Marcia Heiman is Director, Learning to Learn Program, Boston College, Chestnut Hill, Massachusetts. Joshua Slomianko is Co-Director, Learning Skills Consultants, Cambridge, Massachusetts.

INTRODUCTION

Throughout the nation, there is growing interest among language arts teachers and content teachers in teaching for understanding. As a result of this movement, teachers—and especially language arts teachers—are devoting less time to isolated skills instruction. Increasingly, they are teaching thinking and integrating language arts skills in order to improve student understanding of specific works of literature. Additionally, there is growing interest among content teachers in teaching language arts skills (especially reading comprehension and writing) across the curriculum as a means to understanding the information in content courses. With this flourishing of interest, there arises the need for frameworks that can be used to integrate the language arts and to teach thinking across the curriculum.

However, the instructional approaches in many schools do not specify teaching thinking, integrating the language arts, or relating skills directly to the content of a novel or essay (5). We perceive that many teachers and administrators are searching for methods to teach skills that reflect the new research on thinking, teaching for understanding, and instruction in the language arts and in content areas.

PURPOSE OF THE BOOK

The purpose of this book is to present a framework that language arts and content teachers can use to address both the thrust to teach reading, writing, listening, and speaking as a means to understanding and the need for skills instruction that reflects recent research. In particular, our framework conceptualizes learning as the process of assimilating new ideas within the context of specific learning goals. This framework integrates research on learning and instruction in each of the language arts as well as research on the organizational patterns found in literature and content texts. Three major themes pervade this research and are emphasized throughout this book: (1) the learner works actively to construct meaning in each of the language arts areas, (2) the goals of instruction involve both understanding the content in meaningful ways and becoming an independent learner, and (3) a key to both goals is learning how to link the new information to prior knowledge.

The instructional strategies used throughout this book have emerged largely from current research in thinking and have been documented to be effective in the classroom. Some of these strategies emphasize modeling specific thought processes by thinking aloud, providing explicit strategy instruction, and gradually reducing the amount of teacher direction so that students take responsibility for their own learning. Other strategies relate to teaching students to use organizational patterns and graphic outlining or mapping, both as a means of comprehension and as an aid to writing and speaking. These strategies and concepts define the parameters of what we call *cognitive instruction* (59; see also 90).

Our goal in developing this framework for cognitive instruction is to help classroom teachers as well as administrators and curriculum specialists. Toward this end, we provide three Planning Guides, one at the end of each of the research chapters (Chapters 1–3), and five extended examples (Chapters 4 and 5) that can be used to plan for classroom instruction. Our examples include objectives for literature selections, communication skills, and the content passages in basal readers. Three of the examples are content-driven in that the instruction focuses on learning specific strategies and skills as a means to learning the content objectives. Two of the examples involve skills instruction that reflects current thought on thinking and instruction.

This difference in emphasis on content and skills objectives reflects our strong preference for content-driven instruction wherever possible. However, we recognize that sometimes it is not possible for individual teachers to provide such instruction if the school's objectives require mastery of specific skills. Moreover, we provide evidence throughout Part 1 that low-achieving students may benefit from explicit strategy instruction and information about organizational patterns.

ORGANIZATION OF THE BOOK

The book is organized into two parts. Part 1 presents the framework for teaching the language arts as thinking; the topics covered are learning, organizational patterns, and instruction. It is in Part 1 that our essential concept—strategic teaching—is defined. In Part 2, we present five examples for teaching specific content and skills objectives. These examples can be used as models for sequencing instruction for both language arts and content area objectives; because they were developed from the Planning Guides in Part 1, they embody the guidelines regarding learning, organizational patterns, and instruction outlined there.

Uses for the Framework

The framework presented here may be used by both content area teachers and language arts teachers at elementary, middle, and high

8

school levels. Additionally, we hope that teachers, instructional supervisors and resource staff, and curriculum specialists can work together to implement strategic teaching in various subject areas and grade levels throughout a school or district. Our framework for strategic teaching is cohesive, yet robust, providing teachers with many options and guidelines to apply broadly. This flexibility is vital because each learning situation has some unique characteristics. At the same time, we see a need for a framework that provides a common philosophy and knowledge base so that the cooperating partners share a common language. Thus, this framework could provide the basis for developing curriculum and instruction in a school or district and still provide teachers at every grade level with choices and research-based ideas to apply to their unique situations.

Note: In keeping with the recent interest in classroom research and the teacher as researcher, we have included numerous references for further investigation. Generally, we have tried, wherever possible, to select references that have direct implications for classroom instruction. Additionally, we have included a glossary of terms, not only because some terms may be unfamiliar, but also because even familiar terms may have nuances of meaning in research that are not associated with their common meanings.

We hope that those already involved in research-based efforts to teach thinking will treat this book as a good friend, anticipating the general perspective perhaps, but looking forward to fresh insight and information updates. For those who have been less involved in this research, we hope this book will be exciting and informative. Above all, we hope that our readers will find it practical for application to classroom instruction.

Part 1

LEARNING AND INSTRUCTION

Two ideas have guided the development of the framework we describe in Part 1. First, we have assumed that instructional approaches must be firmly grounded in what is known about thinking and learning. Most of the research cited here emerges from cognitive psychology—and especially from research on reading and writing and research on organizational patterns. Second, most of the time spent in schools involves textual materials in some way: reading them, discussing them, listening to information about them, and generating student "texts" in writing. For this reason, our framework is primarily for text-based instruction; it focuses on teaching the thinking processes in reading, writing, listening, and speaking in order to help students to understand the various texts that are presented in schools and to express their ideas in writing and speaking.

Chapter 1 describes a number of *parallel concepts shared by research on reading, writing, listening, and speaking*. Particularly important are the focus on constructing meaning and the notion that the learner is strategic, working actively to link the new information to prior knowledge and drawing on a repertoire of thinking strategies. Some of these strategies are used to process information; others are used to monitor the thinking process itself. Also important is the theme throughout this chapter and the book that learning is recursive (recurring) and nonlinear—that is, the learner continually returns to earlier thoughts for revision as new information is understood and assimilated. Finally, we try to reconcile the notion that thinking is recursive and nonlinear with the fact that thinking takes place in three more or less distinct phases within a specific learning situation. Thus, before focused learning there is some period of preparation or preliminary thinking. This period is followed by "on-line processing" (efforts to process each segment as it is perceived) during focused learning. After focused learning there is a period of consolidation and application. The thinking strategies used during these three phases of learning are summarized in the Planning Guide at the end of the chapter.

Chapter 2 discusses *the uses of organizational patterns*, such as compare/contrast, that are found in virtually all subject matter texts as well as in student writing. We argue that variations of these same patterns can also be found in speech. Then we discuss questioning and graphic outlining techniques that use these organizational patterns to help students to understand "the big picture" in spoken and written texts. This chapter concludes with a Planning Guide that summarizes typical questions and categories of information associated with these organizational patterns.

Chapter 3 presents the heart of this book—the concept of *strategic teaching*, the counterpart of the concept of strategic learning. Strategic teaching is the notion that the teacher has a repertoire of instructional strategies that he or she draws upon to help students to think about what they read and hear as well as what they produce when they write and speak. These strategies are designed to achieve two broad learning goals: to help students to link new information to prior knowledge and to help students to become independent learners in each phase of a learning episode.

Chapter 3 concludes with a Planning Guide that summarizes key instructional strategies for each phase of learning from text. This guide integrates the instructional strategies presented both in Chapter 2, on using organizational patterns to help students focus and organize their thinking, and in Chapter 3, on strategic teaching. Teachers and curriculum specialists can use this guide to select specific strategies for objectives in literature courses; skills instruction in reading, writing, listening, and speaking; and the content passages in basal readers and other reading materials.

The key concepts and even the Planning Guides in Part 1 are working ideas. They have evolved from the previous research of others and ourselves, and they are still evolving in terms of applications in the content areas (62). Thus, this book is essentially a photograph of current research and its implications for classroom instruction for the language arts, including the content passages found in basal readers.

Chapter 1

THE LANGUAGE ARTS
AS THINKING PROCESSES

Current research on reading has provided much insight into the process of comprehending. There are parallel findings in recent research on writing, listening, and speaking. We believe that these similarities exist because all of these thinking processes are merely "different realizations of the same language system" (103, p. 116).

THE "NEW" DEFINITION OF READING

Comprehension as Thinking

Constructing Meaning: Traditionally, it has been assumed that knowledge is acquired largely through decoding. In contrast, cognitive psychology defines comprehension as an interaction of the reader, the features of the text, and the context in which the message is given (5). Meaning is not contained in the words, nor is it revealed by decoding them. Rather, the effective reader works actively to construct meaning from the whole text, taking into account contextual factors such as the purpose for reading and the information given by the teacher. In this view, comprehension is fundamentally goal oriented—the goals being to understand, to retain, and to apply information.

The phrase "construct meaning from text" pervades research on reading. Stated most simply, to construct meaning from text means to think about what is read, to make inferences about what is not stated explicitly, and to integrate what is learned with what is already known. However, this process is quite complex and involves various cognitive activities before, during, and after sustained reading. Further, this process ultimately involves developing concepts and, in certain instances, changing misconceptions (3).

Constructing meaning from text is hardly a new idea. Good teachers have been helping students to do this throughout the years. In fact, researchers have spent considerable time deriving models of instruction from what good teachers do. We refer here to the "new" definition of reading for two reasons. First, this definition is in contrast to the "old" definition that stressed decoding almost exclusively. What is *new* about the new definition of reading is specification of the thinking processes used for knowledge acquisition and conceptual change. This specification is important because a number of these processes are often either not taught in schools or not taught effectively (36). Second, "the new definition of reading" is a grass-roots phrase used by teachers, administrators, and decision makers in schools and states that are implementing programs based on recent research in reading.

Linking the New Information to Prior Knowledge: What are the thinking processes utilized to construct meaning? While there are many ways to answer this question, we look first to schema theory.* According to such schema theorists as R. C. Anderson (4), information is stored in memory in knowledge structures or schemata, which are like mental file folders. Besides containing information, schemata permit the learner to assimilate new ideas by determining what is important, making inferences, and elaborating on the meaning of what is read.

To explain how the proficient reader uses these knowledge structures, we have drawn a composite picture from several descriptions. Those offered by A. Collins, J. S. Brown, and K. M. Larkin (26), P. D. Pearson and M. C. Gallagher (86), H. Singer and D. Donlan (100), R. J. Spiro and A. Myers (101), and R. J. Tierney (105) may be particularly helpful to teachers.

The proficient reader begins the comprehension process by skimming parts of the text and/or by considering information provided by the teacher. Following these thinking activities, the model reader formulates hypotheses about the meaning and organization of the text. The good reader then uses these hypotheses to activate his or her knowledge about the content and organizational patterns of the text. At some point, the good reader may also review his or her reading/thinking strategies.

In this context, the word *activate* means much more than recall or review. Activating prior knowledge is a highly selective, interpretive, and often largely unconscious process in good readers. It involves scanning various mental files, selecting bits of relevant information from several sources, and making inferences about how the bits are related to each other and to the text. These inferences are then used to make predictions about the meaning and the organizational pattern of the text and about strategies for comprehending it.

Schema is the singular of schemata or knowledge structures.

As reading progresses, the reader continually confirms, modifies, or rejects the initial hypotheses and evaluates the effectiveness of the strategies selected. To do this, the reader must constantly interact with the text, asking what is important and unimportant, formulating hypotheses about how ideas are related, and comparing new information to prior knowledge—sometimes recalling additional information from memory, sometimes altering past conceptions, sometimes disagreeing with the author, sometimes anticipating content to come, and sometimes relegating unneeded bits of information back to storage. This process of revision and refinement is inherently a "start/pause," nonlinear process, with pauses for reflection as well as efforts to look ahead in the text or review what has been read. This process may also involve efforts to represent the text, either mentally or graphically, in such ways as semantic mapping and graphic outlining.

It is evident from this description that thinking is fundamentally recursive and nonlinear, with numerous efforts both to "loop back" to earlier thoughts to accommodate new ideas and to anticipate what is to come and/or skip ahead in the text. At the same time, it is also evident that reading takes place in phases. Before reading, the model reader engages various thinking processes to activate (recall) prior knowledge and to formulate hypotheses about the meaning, both of which serve to focus attention. During reading, numerous thinking processes (including some of those used earlier) are used to comprehend segments of information such as a paragraph or section. After reading, the model reader reflects on the text as a whole and seeks to consolidate or extend learning in various ways.

Strategic Learning as Thinking

The Repertoire of Strategies and Skills: As suggested above, the proficient reader is not only constructive but also planful and strategic. Descriptions of *strategic learning*, a phrase coined by S. G. Paris, M. Y. Lipson, and K. Wixson (85), suggest that the model reader has a repertoire of strategies and skills that he or she draws upon to achieve different purposes and to attain various learning goals (20, 54, 108, 112).

Our interpretation of this body of research on reading skills, strategy instruction, and learning from text is that this repertoire is essentially a "pool" concept. We believe that the skilled reader draws upon her or his knowledge of strategies and skills in this pool in much the same way that she or he draws upon knowledge of content. To explain, as the skilled reader begins to get some idea of the substance and scope of the reading task, she or he scans the mental file folders that comprise this repertoire and selects knowledge of appropriate strategies to call up from long-term memory for use in the present learning situation. As the task progresses, the proficient reader continually monitors the hypothesis that the strategies recalled are indeed the ones that best apply to the task or problem.

Types of Strategies: Most researchers refer to two broad categories of strategies in this repertoire: cognitive and metacognitive. Cognitive strategies are the thinking processes and skills described above that the reader uses to process information and construct meaning. M. Pressley, J. G. Borkowski, and W. Schneider (88) identify two types of strategies that we would call cognitive strategies. First, there are *goal-specific strategies*, such as categorizing a list of ideas or concepts in order to understand their relationship. Second, there are *higher-order strategies*, which are really clusters or sequences of strategies—for example, previewing a text, generating predictions, reading to confirm them, and summarizing. Higher-order strategies differ from goal-specific strategies in that higher-order strategies are oriented toward in-depth understanding.

Metacognition means literally "above" cognition or thinking. Essentially, metacognition refers to knowing how, when, and where to apply a given strategy as well as to persisting in one's efforts to achieve learning goals (19, 81, 88). Metacognition has two dimensions: awareness and control. That is, the model reader thinks about his or her own learning processes and tries to control them. Metacognitive activities that facilitate comprehension include the following: (1) clarifying (asking a teacher or a classmate to help to define a word or a relationship), (2) verifying (raising questions about the adequacy of the information), (3) evaluating new ideas and testing them against prior knowledge, (4) struggling with contradictions and inconsistencies, (5) revising earlier thoughts, and (6) withholding judgment. Other factors—commitments of time and energy, motivation and interest, and beliefs about responsibility for learning throughout the learning process—relate to the learner's efforts to persist in achieving learning goals. Thinking about learning goals, planning what strategies to use, evaluating their effectiveness, and learning how and when to apply them to new situations are also critical metacognitive strategies.

To summarize briefly, much of reading research focuses on two key ideas: the best learning occurs when the reader works actively to construct meaning from text, and the model reader is a strategic learner, drawing upon a repertoire or pool of strategies. This repertoire includes cognitive strategies, such as mentally reviewing prior knowledge in order to integrate new information, and metacognitive (monitoring) strategies, such as clarifying and revising to think about and control the learning process. The specification of these cognitive and metacognitive strategies is important because many of them are not specified explicitly in tradi-

15

tional school curriculums for the language arts or for content courses. It is also important to understand that metacognitive strategies constantly interact with cognitive strategies throughout the various phases of constructing meaning.

Other characteristics of thinking seem somewhat contradictory. On the one hand, the process of comprehending occurs in phases before, during, and after reading. On the other hand, thinking is fundamentally recursive and nonlinear. Thus, any thinking process, such as formulating questions, may occur in all phases, and there is a constant effort to "loop back" to earlier thoughts to evaluate and revise them. We will return to this apparent contradiction below.

PARALLEL CONCEPTS IN WRITING

Current research on writing has numerous parallels to reading research. While it is not within the scope of this book to document all the parallels between reading and writing, we will discuss briefly several that pertain to our framework. As with reading, our composite description of the writing process is drawn from several research descriptions; those of A. N. Applebee (9), C. R. Cooper and A. Matsuhashi (27), K. Duckworth and W. D. Bevoise (34), L. Flower and J. R. Hayes (40), D. H. Graves (46), and M. Scardamalia and C. Bereiter (94) were particularly helpful.

Parallels in Constructing Meaning

First, both reading and writing are goal oriented, the goal being to construct meaningful messages using different genres. Second, a common thread throughout writing research is the notion that the expert writer actively seeks to construct meaningful messages. Thus, composing is essentially an interaction among the writer, the text that she or he generates, and the context, especially the audience. Moreover, prior knowledge of content, or domain-specific knowledge, clearly plays a critical role in this interaction, as is the case in reading. Third, composing is a complex process involving various subprocesses. Most writing researchers refer to the following: prewriting or planning, monitoring, drafting, revising, and editing. Fourth, composing is highly recursive, involving each of these subprocesses throughout the process of generating a product.

Finally, while writing researchers typically do not conceptualize these subprocesses as operating in specific phases (largely because of this recursive characteristic), it would seem that the process of composing takes

16

place in phases that are analogous to the phases of learning from text. Interestingly, whereas much of the emphasis in reading research is on the before and after phases, most of writing research discusses what takes place during focused writing. Thus, they are not directly parallel in this regard. However, we believe that it is fruitful for planning instruction to conceptualize the process of generating a written product in terms of three phases—before focused writing, during focused writing, and after focused writing—recognizing that each phase contains recurring cycles of planning, drafting, evaluating, and revising.

The Process of Composing

In the prewriting phase (before focused writing), the expert writer engages in a variety of activities in order to select information from prior knowledge that relates to the task. Especially important during this phase is the selection of content information, writing plan, audience, and goals for segments of text as well as for the product as a whole. This scanning of mental file folders may yield a rich lode of ideas which the proficient writer must sort, prioritize, and organize in some way. Once prior knowledge is activated, there may be any number of cycles of monitoring and revising the initial plan and the information recalled. This prewriting phase may also involve some effort to take notes, to construct graphic representations, or even to generate some preliminary sketches of specific segments in much the same way that the reader may make some preliminary hypotheses about or representations of the text to come. Thus, prewriting, like prereading, may involve some preliminary engagement in writing and reading respectively, but not a sustained effort.

During sustained writing, the proficient writer works actively to draft ideas that reflect the plan laid out in the prewriting phase. However, this phase is highly recursive in that the expert writer is constantly evaluating the current text, modifying his or her message by rejecting or modifying previously stated ideas and wording, translating the message into different language, considering how the audience will respond, selecting different information from prior knowledge, and establishing new points of emphasis. Thus, throughout this phase, the good writer continually compares the text produced at any given moment to his or her representation of the audience's perspective, to previously written text, to prior knowledge, and to anticipated subsequent text. These points of comparison may include any or all of the following: topic, vocabulary, syntax, and organizational pattern.

Eventually, there is a moment in which the proficient writer feels that she or he is ready to release the draft for some phase of final editing.

17

This last editing and revision may focus on such things as syntax, word meaning, and sentence-level considerations as well as on overall meaning and organizational patterns. This revision phase may be brief, involving only minimal planning, selecting, and drafting—or it may be quite lengthy, if substantial problems are uncovered. Indeed, the writer may reject the product more or less completely and start over again.

Not surprisingly, given the similarities between reading and writing, there is now an increasing body of literature on the reading/writing relationship. P. D. Pearson and R. J. Tierney (87), for example, have gained much insight into the process of reading by conceptualizing the reader as a writer composing a message. Additionally, there are important implications from text analysis for writing (see below).

The Repertoire of Writing Strategies

Another parallel between reading and writing is the notion that the expert writer is strategic and planful. Apparently, student writers conceptualize writing as "knowledge telling," according to M. Scardamalia and C. Bereiter (94); they "tell" what they know about a topic and stop when they have nothing more to say, with little planning or thought about strategies and organizational patterns. In contrast, expert writers use various strategies including writing plans and organizational patterns (71, 72). Expert writers also use various monitoring strategies to revise their goals and their texts. Thus, the expert writer also has a repertoire of writing strategies and skills for each of the subprocesses listed above.

PARALLEL CONCEPTS IN LISTENING AND SPEAKING

Given that listening and reading both involve comprehending and that speaking and writing usually both involve some degree of composing, it seems likely that the underlying cognitive and metacognitive processes are closely parallel in many ways. Yet, it is important to note from the outset of this discussion that, due to constraints of space and our focus in this book, we cannot address the abundance of research on informal speaking and listening as it occurs in fluid dialogues and other contexts. Thus, our discussion in this section will be limited to the research on listening comprehension, such as listening to lectures and stories, and instances of speaking associated with argumentation, which is a type of text, according to our definition of text. Below we consider models of listening and argumentation separately; then we will consider some common parallels.

18

Listening Comprehension

P. Friedman (42), for example, defines the listening process in terms of three phases: attention (the before phase), understanding (the during phase), and evaluation (the after phase). A. D. Wolvin and C. G. Coakley (114) have devised a somewhat more complex model of listening: the listener responds to a stimulus that she or he receives (the before phase), attends to it with meaning assigned (the during phase), and remembers, acts on, or evaluates it with feedback of some kind (the after phase).

S. W. Lundsteen's model (66) of the listening process is interesting because she discusses the role of prior knowledge and the cognitive processes of the model learner for each phase of listening. The learner must (1) hear the stimulus and (2) hold it in memory before (3) he/she can attend to the message. Once the message is perceived, the learner (4) forms images of the meaning of the message, (5) searches for past stored ideas, (6) compares the incoming information to the prior knowledge, scanning for organizational cues, (7) tests the hypothesized meaning by looking for additional cues and a good "match" between the incoming information and the hypothesized meaning, (8) recodes the information according to the meaning, (9) stores the information, and (10) thinks beyond listening, using the information for some specific purpose such as problem solving or critical evaluation.

Throughout this conceptualization, Lundsteen emphasizes the recursive nature of the various steps and the variety of higher-order thinking processes needed by the learner to become proficient in listening. There is also the concept of the strategic learner. Indeed, her model contains a lengthy set of complex thinking processes involved in listening.

Argumentation

Models of argumentation, which derive largely from research on speech and communication, indicate that formal speech involves thought processes similar to those underlying the other language arts. J. G. Delia (30), for example, discusses the constructivist position. Essentially, communication is defined in terms of constructing meaning. That is, the individual works actively to perceive and interpret the reality of what is stated. According to C. L. Hale (47), another argumentation researcher, the data for this "sense-making" process are the verbal and nonverbal cues perceived by the individual, but the sense-making itself is interpretation, and the role that prior knowledge plays in this process is critical. Additionally, the proficient learner is armed with specific argumentation strategies for developing and evaluating an argument. G. B. LaFleur (63), for example, defines nine specific strategies to resolve an argu-

19

ment—among them are bolstering, exploding, refusing, and redefining.

S. Toulmin (107) has devised a generic model that defines the essential elements of argumentation in terms of the following seven concepts: claims, ground, warrants, backing, model, qualifiers, and rebuttal. This model is intended to provide a common language for educators to use across the curriculum for teaching argumentation.

PARALLELS AMONG READING, WRITING, LISTENING, AND SPEAKING

First, like reading and writing research, both listening and speaking research defines the underlying thinking processes as goal oriented, the goal being to construct or communicate meaning. Second, there is an emphasis on the importance of prior knowledge, though it does not seem to be emphasized as strongly as it is in reading and writing. Third, the process of constructing meaning in listening and speaking is often conceptualized explicitly or implicitly in terms of three phases that closely parallel our concept of the three phases in reading and writing. Fourth, while the process of presenting a story or argument may be highly linear, the process of listening comprehension is recursive and nonlinear as are the processes of constructing a speech or argument and of analyzing it. Finally, both listening and speaking share the concept of strategic learning, either implicitly or explicitly, along with reading and writing. That is, both cognitive and metacognitive strategies appear to be involved in listening and speaking. Thus, it seems that there are close parallels in the thinking processes in all four language arts areas.

IMPLICATIONS FOR INSTRUCTION

We began this chapter indicating that we anticipated finding numerous parallels in reading, writing, listening, and speaking because all of these processes were "realizations of the same language system." The body of this chapter has teased out both the diversity of these processes and some of the specific ways in which they are similar. Now we must ask, "What are the implications for instruction?"

Two broad issues are critical. First, we need to show how all of the different processes relate. This means providing a framework that integrates the language arts as well as metacognitive and cognitive processes. Second, we need to develop a concept of sequencing instruction that simultaneously accounts for the recursive and nonlinear quality of thinking and also for the notion that thinking progresses through phases in any given learning situation.

20

The key to addressing both criteria is the language used to describe the three phases of learning because this language will drive the sequence of instruction for any given learning situation. This language becomes even more important when we consider some of the more "impoverished" notions of lesson plans.

Most lesson plans are organized around a specific objective that becomes the *focal point* of learning: a concept, a generalization or universal truth, and so on. Moreover, most lesson plans organize instructional activities into before, during, and after phases around this focal point. What is impoverished is the quality of instruction that is planned for each phase. These lesson plans do not focus on understanding the meaning as the ultimate goal of learning. They may not account for the interaction of cognitive and metacognitive strategies needed during each phase to accomplish that goal. Nor is it likely that they will provide for the nonlinear and recursive quality of thinking in each phase. In fact, there are references to lessons in the classroom and in textbooks that consist largely of preteaching difficult vocabulary, presenting some information to be learned, and asking questions to assess what has been learned (5).

We have struggled to provide labels for each phase of learning that will suggest the nature of the thinking processes without implying that learning is linear or unidimensional. Toward this end, we propose the following labels: (1) *preparation*, which involves thinking processes such as defining the task/audience/purpose, planning, activating prior knowledge, anticipating what is to come, and setting specific learning goals; (2) *on-line processing* (processing in segments), which seeks to construct meaning for segments of a poem, a student essay, a lecture, or an argument through recurring cycles that focus on linking new information to prior knowledge; and (3) *consolidation/extension*, which focuses on understanding "the big picture" (i.e., the overall ideas in the poem, essay, etc.), integrating this understanding with prior knowledge, and applying this understanding to new situations.

The various thinking strategies that are involved in these phases are summarized in Planning Guide 1. This guide is an adaptation of a model initially developed for the Association for Supervision and Curriculum Development (82), and it is important to reiterate here that this conceptualization is a working framework that continues to evolve. As such, it is not intended to be comprehensive or definitive; rather, it is intended to suggest our "best-shot" candidates for a list of key thinking processes in the language arts. Thus, what is presented in Planning Guide 1 is essentially a broad-stroke sketch of the thinking processes in the phases of learning in a specific situation. We hope that teachers and curriculum specialists will adapt the language in this guide to reflect their own concepts of the thinking processes in reading, writing, listening, and speaking.

Planning Guide 1 contains two columns. The first column lists the key thinking activities used by the proficient learner at various times to prepare for focused learning and to process the various segments of what is read, written, heard, or spoken. It is critical to note that while all of these processes can be used in some learning situations, it is unlikely that the learner will use all of these activities for lost learning situations. The right column has blank spaces in which to outline a sequence of instructional strategies for before, during, and after focused learning.

The conceptualization of learning in this guide is consistent with a number of models of learning emerging from cognitive psychology and instructional design. This framework is also consistent with our observations of what good teachers think about learning as well as with the new research on expert teaching (17, 64). We believe that a good understanding of learning is fundamental to strategic teaching.

Planning Guide 1

Thinking Processes in the Language Arts*

Thinking Process	Instructional Strategies
PREPARATORY PROCESSING	**BEFORE FOCUSED INSTRUCTION**
Comprehend objective/task Define learning objectives Consider task/audience Determine criteria for success	
Preview/Select materials/cues at hand Skim features and graphic aids Determine content focus/organizational pattern	
Activate prior knowledge Access content and vocabulary Access categories and structure Access strategies/plans	
Focus interest/Set purpose Form hypotheses and questions/Make predictions Represent/Organize ideas (Categorize/Outline)	
ON-LINE PROCESSING (Text Segments)	**DURING FOCUSED INSTRUCTION**
Modify hypotheses/Clarify ideas Check hypotheses, predictions, questions Compare to prior knowledge Ask clarification questions Examine logic of argument, flow of ideas Generate new questions	
Integrate ideas Select important concepts/words Connect and organize ideas, summarize	
Assimilate new ideas Articulate changes in knowledge Evaluate ideas/products Withhold judgment	
CONSOLIDATING/EXTENDING **("The Big Picture")**	**AFTER FOCUSED INSTRUCTION**
Integrate/Organize meaning for whole Categorize and integrate information, conclude Summarize key ideas and connections Evaluate/Revise/Edit	
Assess achievement of purpose/learning Compare new learnings to prior knowledge Identify gaps in learning and information Generate new questions/next steps	
Extend learning Translate/Apply to new situations Rehearse and study	

*Adapted from *Teaching Reading as Thinking* (82). Reprinted with permission.

Chapter 2

THE IMPORTANCE OF ORGANIZATIONAL PATTERNS

In Chapter 1, as we discussed the various thinking processes used in comprehending and composing texts, we touched on the importance of understanding organizational patterns in texts. In this chapter, we discuss the characteristics of the organizational patterns in reading, writing, listening, and speaking. The purpose of this chapter parallels that of Chapter 1. Here, we show that the organizational patterns in each of the language arts are essentially the same. Additionally, we discuss how teachers can use these patterns to help students organize information in reading and writing. Knowledge of these organizational patterns, as well as knowledge of how, when, and where to use them, is a key element in the repertoire of strategies acquired by the model learner. Therefore, knowledge of the nature and use of these patterns should be part of the repertoire of instructional strategies of the strategic teacher.

ORGANIZATIONAL PATTERNS IN WRITTEN, SPOKEN, AND GRAPHIC TEXTS

Organizational Patterns in Written Texts

An organizational pattern is a recognizable arrangement of information. Organizational patterns such as compare/contrast are often called *text structures*. However, the term *organizational pattern* is used here because it is more widely used in schools and because we believe that these patterns extend well beyond texts. In a word, they are fundamental to thinking itself, as suggested above.

Three features of organizational patterns pertain to this discussion. First, there are two types of organizational patterns: *generic* and *specific*. Second, organizational patterns usually contain *signal words* or *text markers* that suggest particular organizational patterns. Third, there are specific questions and categories, called *frames*, that can be used to define and organize the information in a given organizational pattern. Each of these features will be discussed below.

Generic and Specific Patterns: Generic organizational patterns are those that typically cut across texts in literature, science, and other disciplines. Common generic patterns have been described by Meyer (72) and Armbruster (10), each using somewhat different terminology. Ours is a composite list in which we distinguish three different categories of organizational patterns.

First, some organizational patterns focus on one important element or idea, plus supporting information. Within this category, we include descriptive texts, proposition/support patterns such as an opinion paragraph or a text with major and minor ideas, and simple argumentation.

Second, there are organizational patterns that describe sequences of something. These patterns include temporal structures such as a series of events, steps in a procedure, and stages of development, as well as the goal/action/outcome pattern.

Third, other patterns emphasize two or more focal points, plus sequential elements in some instances. These include compare/contrast, problem/solution, cause/effect, and interaction of two or more persons or groups.

Content-specific organizational patterns are recognizable arrangements of ideas that are found in specific-content texts. Story grammars are content-specific patterns, for example. *Story grammar* refers to the actual structure of a story as well as to the knowledge of that structure that the learner brings to bear in reading or listening to a story (102). This knowledge can consist of simple notions about stories having a beginning, middle, and end. Or it can include knowledge of specific genres such as legends and autobiographies, as well as techniques used to attain mood and style (10). We believe that the recent thrust to study content knowledge and content texts will reveal other content-specific organizational patterns.

Text Markers and Signal Words: As stated earlier, a second feature of organizational patterns is the use of text markers and signal words. In well-written prose texts, both generic and content-specific patterns are highlighted by key words and phrases which serve as cues to the reader in identifying a particular organizational pattern (33, 54, 70). Thus, when the reader sees such a phrase as "in contrast," he or she can predict that the organizational pattern is compare/contrast. Text markers for sequential texts include "at first," "eventually," and "after." Regarding content-specific patterns, the use of such phrases as "once upon a time" in children's stories, animal characters in folk tales, and references to specific time periods in historical novels signals the reader about specific genre

25

patterns. Skills Example 1 in Chapter 5 includes an extensive list of these signal words for generic organizational patterns.

Frame Questions and Categories: Frames are a third feature of organizational patterns. Frames are sets of questions and categories used to specify and "chunk" information within generic and content-specific organizational patterns. These chunks may be arranged in various ways, depending on the organizational pattern and the meaning constructed by the composer or comprehender.

Consider the frame questions for the problem/solution pattern (a generic pattern):

- Who had the problem?
- What was the problem?
- What caused this problem?
- What were the negative effects?
- What actions were taken to solve the problem?
- What were the results of these actions?

These particular questions were used to integrate information about the national debt and other problems in a social studies text (58).

Authors often have such questions in mind when writing a textbook, even if they do not state them explicitly. However, even if frame questions are not stated, a good reader knows and uses them to organize and enhance her or his understanding of the problem and solution.

Frame categories function in the same way. Numerous researchers have discussed the categories that are needed to understand concepts (68). Specifically, in order to understand a vocabulary term or concept in literature or any other content area, it is important to know the definition, the critical features, the domain or category, examples, and, where appropriate, nonexamples. Good descriptions of a concept that include the information in most of those categories are rare in literature. However, a good learner tries to gather this information or to generate it by inference. A good teacher also relates the new concept to prior knowledge in some way.

Because generic patterns cut across the various content areas, the specific frame questions and categories may vary somewhat. The problem-solving frame referred to above, for instance, would have different questions for solving a problem in science or conceptualizing a character's problem in a literary work. Similarly, the specific categories for a proposition/support text structure may vary greatly, depending on the age of the student and the course. In elementary school, most textbooks refer simply to two categories: main ideas and details. With older students, there are additional categories for the proposition/support pattern: major ideas, minor ideas, and details. This same organizational pattern takes yet other forms as students learn about writing themes and thesis statements.

Planning Guide 2 contains frame questions and categories for generic organizational patterns. Figures 1, 2, and 3 illustrate how three different frames apply to specific examples. (For easy reference, we have placed all of the figures in this chapter at the end.) However, we will defer discussion of Planning Guide 2 and the figures until later.

Content-specific frames, as the name implies, are found only in a particular content area. B. B. Armbruster and T. H. Anderson (11; see also 10), for example, refer to the region frame that is common in most geography texts but rarely found in other texts. This frame contains such categories as land surface features, bodies of water, climate, and population characteristics. Thus, the region frame is essentially a descriptive organizational pattern.

Similarly, the government frame, containing questions to establish who governs and what the rights of the people are, would be found in any number of social science texts or historical novels but not in science texts. Texts for the physical sciences are likely to contain patterns to describe processes such as photosynthesis and parts of complex systems such as the lungs (67).

Organizational Patterns in Spoken Texts

T. G. Devine (32) posits that the word *text* includes any verbal utterance that is seen or heard, a position we have taken throughout this book and elsewhere (61). Given this premise, we would argue that speech often contains the same organizational patterns as prose text. Consider the teacher who is explaining a plot. His or her explanation may well reflect (implicitly or explicitly) the frame questions, categories, and signal words of a problem/solution text, a sequential text, or an interaction text. Or consider the compare/contrast example above. One would surely expect to hear the teacher use such signal words as "however," "in contrast," "similarities," "differences," and so on. Similarly, a spoken text such as a lecture, a teacher explanation, or a debate would contain the same frame questions and categories as the same content in print. These parallels exist because, as noted earlier, the spoken word is a manifestation of the same language system as the printed text.

Organizational Patterns in Graphic Texts

Graphics include the variety of illustrations found in textbooks and other instructional materials. Graphic texts may or may not use words to signal a specific pattern, but it is evident that they reflect particular organizational patterns. Pictures and diagrams, for example, reflect a descriptive pattern or structure. Semantic maps may also be used to portray various organizational patterns such as description and concept/definition or concept hierarchies. Time lines and flowcharts are different types of sequential text structures. Tables and charts reflect compare-and-contrast text structures. Text markers and other structural information are given in the captions, labels, arrows, lines, legends, symbols, and other features of graphic texts.

Additionally, B. F. Jones, and others (61) argue that graphic and prose texts have important characteristics in common. That is, well-written prose texts have well-defined organizational patterns, including the use of frames and signal words, clear connections among ideas, and vocabulary appropriate to the audience (7). These criteria are used to develop and evaluate prose texts, and Jones and her colleagues have shown that they can also be used to analyze graphic texts. L. B. Friedman and M. Tinzmann (41) have used these criteria to evaluate the graphics in social studies texts; their research suggests that graphics are arranged in terms of the same organizational patterns as prose because graphics are representations of ideas and information that we express and comprehend through language.

FRAMES AND GRAPHIC OUTLINES
FOR ORGANIZING THINKING

The Effects of Well-Organized Prose on Comprehension and Recall

There is now a growing body of research on how students respond to different types of text structures in prose texts. Apparently, even very young readers are aware of and use structural information to organize their recollections of what they read (102). This use of structural information in the text not only increases the amount recalled but also improves long-term retention (74). Further, recall is greater when the text contains closely knit patterns such as compare/contrast as compared to more open-ended patterns such as description.

Interestingly, whether a text is well organized and well signaled or poorly written can have a significant impact on the amount recalled as well as on the organization of recall (97). Additionally, good readers impose their perceptions of the author's text structure on recall, whether the author's text is well signaled or not. However, poor readers tend not to have well-organized recall except when the author's organizational pattern is well signaled (73). In effect, well-written text or "considerate text," to use a phrase coined by T. H. Anderson and B. B. Armbruster (8), has the potential to improve the organizational patterns of poor readers when they write.

S. M. Shimmerlik (97) also indicates that merely providing content-specific cues or prompts at the time of recall significantly improved both recall and organization of recall of prose text. In most instances, these cues were single words such as category labels for the points of comparison in a comparative text. These labels functioned as frame categories and greatly facilitated chunking the information. B. F. Jones reports an anecdote in which she embedded these categorical cues in essay questions for a group of upper elementary students and obtained unexpectedly good results, according to their respective teachers (60).

Thus, the organizational patterns in texts play an important role in comprehension and written recall. Evidence that students can be taught to use the structural information in organizaitonal patterns is discussed in the next section.

The Effects of Teaching Students to Use Structural Information

B. F. Jones, M. R. Amiran, and M. Katims (60) examined studies in which students were taught spontaneously (without cues) various learning strategies such as categorizing, outlining, and visualizing. They wanted to discover why some efforts to teach students to use structural information were successful, while others were not. They found that studies that merely directed students to use these strategies were typically less successful than studies that provided structural information about the categories and/or other information about the text. The most significant effects were found in studies that provided this structural information as well as explicit strategy instruction, including modeling how to use the structural information and providing practice with feedback. Frequently, this type of strategy instruction improved writing as well as comprehension and retention (see also 28 and 109).

M. Scardamalia and C. Bereiter (94) discuss the trend in writing research overr the last decade to provide explicit structural information as an intervention in composing. Specifically, they note that students of various ages, including those in the elementary grades, can be taught to recognize and use various types of organizational patterns including arguments (93, 104).

Moreover, there have been numerous efforts to teach students at all levels to use various types of maps and graphic outlines to facilitate comprehension and/or writing. Semantic maps are comprised of words and phrases connected by lines or arrows. Semantic maps may be used to build vocabulary by associating synonyms and other information from the previous experiences of the class as a whole for a given vocabulary term (52). These maps are also used in the form of graphic organizers which summarize information and story maps which show the key ideas.

Idol-Maestas and Croll (51), for example, have taught poor readers to use story-mapping procedures to outline whole stories.

Graphic outlines usually consist of matrices and boxes containing more extended discourse. They are used to outline information in much more detail than semantic maps. D. F. Dansereau (28), for example, has developed a system of graphic outlining for expository prose. He teaches low-achieving college students to use such structural elements as the headings and subheadings within science and other technical texts by constructing complex network maps (24).

Several researchers have taught upper elementary school students to apply compare/contrast frames to texts in various subject areas (89). B. F. Jones and M. R. Amiran have developed a type of graphic outlining called *matrix outlining*, which involves taking notes in tables or matrices and then using the structure of the matrix as the basis for organizing compare/contrast essays (60). This training improved both comprehension and organization of recall and had a limited impact on writing essays.

One reason for the success of these mapping and graphic outlining strategies is that their construction usually involves a high level of interaction between teacher and student, which helps not only in-depth processing but motivation as well (53). As indicated earlier, another reason for their success may be that they encourage nonlinear thinking.

Uses of Structural Information for Instruction

The body of research on organizational patterns suggests that they have various uses. First, text markers and frames can be used to *locate information in written, spoken, and graphic texts*. A student who is aware that an essay involves a problem/solution structure can use that information to locate the description of the problem and the solution. Alternatively, that same information can be used to discover that no solution is given.

Second, maps, frames, and graphic outlines can be used to *organize and integrate information*. For example, if a student recognizes that a text or a teacher is discussing a problem, she or he can recall the problem/solution questions and use them to formulate predictions or questions about the content of the text or discussion. Or suppose that a student has several sources of information about a topic—e.g., an essay, a lecture, and a film with three different viewpoints. In such instances, he or she can learn to use frame questions and categories to integrate the information from the various sources. These uses of frames apply to comprehending written texts as well as oral texts.

Third, maps and graphic outlines *encourage nonlinear thinking.* Any item in the matrix or table, for example, is associated with adjacent items on either side as well as with the column and row headings. Consequently, the reader can analyze more items in relation to each other in graphic outlines than is possible in linear outlining. This capability permits not only generalizations about the information in whole rows and columns but also compare/contrast analysis among the rows and columns. This capability to facilitate nonlinear thinking is highly consistent with the analysis of thinking and learning emphasized in Chapter 1, as is the capability of these graphics to integrate information.

Fourth, signal words, maps, and graphic outlines *facilitate retention* because they provide rich contexts for each bit of information and they encourage chunking in recall. That is, each of the relationships specified by the category labels in a matrix (or by arrows and labels in other types of graphics) serves as a "hook" for the reader to link the new bits of information to each other and to prior knowledge. Even a glance at these figures shows that there are more associations or hooks for each piece of information than in linear outlining. It is also evident that frame questions and categories serve as cues or prompts for organizing information in recall.

Fifth, the various features of organizational patterns may be used to *organize students' written compositions.* M. Scardamalia and C. Bereiter (94, p. 783) use the term *framing* to refer to "the active process of creating and organizing structure for a composition." They argue that most writing researchers share the assumption that "these structures are not merely characterizations that inevitably emerge in text but that they represent knowledge that readers and writers process." Therefore, learning the structural elements in various types of written texts should be a major requirement for competence in writing in schools, according to Scardamalia and Bereiter. We would argue that learning the structural elements of organizational patterns should be a major requirement for competence in reading, listening, and speaking as well. Interestingly, the Michigan State Department of Education's new reading test will require students to be aware of the use of organizational patterns for narrative and expository prose.

Frames are particularly helpful for organizing and evaluating information in both written and spoken compositions. The various frame questions and categories in Planning Guide 2 could be used in the planning stage for an essay or a speech as well as for evaluation and revision of the draft during or after sustained writing. For example, B. F. Jones (58) has developed a scoring procedure in which teachers specify the structural elements they think are appropriate for a given type of essay or paragraph and the criteria for evaluating the quality of the content. These specifications are then shared with the student for purposes of planning and self-evaluation. Additionally, Jones (57) has provided guidelines for developing graphic outlines that reflect the structure of the organizational pattern and may thereby facilitate comprehension.

At this point, we refer the reader again to Figures 1, 2, and 3 at the end of this chapter. Note how the graphic structures reflect the text structure categories and questions. The compare/contrast matrix frame in Figure 1 helps the learner see clearly what is being compared (the two characters) and the categories or points of comparison. The boxes in the interaction frame in Figure 2 help the learner to distinguish among the goals, actions, and outcomes for each of the two characters. The boxes in the problem/solution frame in Figure 3 look quite different because they are devised to distinguish the elements of the problem and the solution. Notice also the rich contextual associations for each item.

Finally, the relationship between the frame categories and questions and the summaries is noteworthy. The teacher can use these to help students construct summaries of their own. However, it is important to recognize that the instruction should be gradual and that students will need much practice. In the initial stages of this instruction, it is important to provide model essays for the students as well as explicit statements explaining the relationship among the boxes in the frame, the frame questions, and the various parts of the summary. Next, teachers may work with the class as a group to construct a summary.

Later, the students may be asked to generate their own summaries. Then questions or categories in the frame may be included in the space for writing the summary. If the concept is very difficult, some of the sentences in the essay may be given as well. As students progress, these questions are gradually eliminated so that students generate their own essays independent of modeling, teacher explanation, and prompts embedded in the text.

This process of gradually shifting the responsibility for learning from the teacher to the student is called *scaffolding*. Chapter 3 and Part 2 contain other examples of this technique; in fact, much of the instruction in Part 2 will demonstrate the use of frames and graphic outlines in scaffolded instruction. We cannot emphasize too strongly how important it is to provide not only the structural information (the frame questions and categories as well as the signal words) but also instruction and practice in how to apply this information. This process takes time and commitment on the part of the teacher. However, we believe that such a commitment is important if students are to develop proficiency in using organizational patterns in various contexts. We also believe that such commitment is fundamental to strategic teaching.

Planning Guide 2

Frames for Generic Organizational Patterns

Texts Containing only One Major Element or Idea and Supporting Information

1. **DESCRIPTION OF ONE THING:** Descriptions of one thing in literature may focus on the characters, places, or objects. In such a description, it is critical to identify the thing being described and its attributes. Descriptive texts are sometimes referred to as *list* or *collection structures* because the attributes may be described in any order. Description in content-area passages may be guided by content-specific frames such as the region frame.

2. **PROPOSITION/SUPPORT:** Proposition/support is a very common paragraph structure. In its simplest form, it is a statement plus information supporting the statement. This structure is difficult to recognize because there are few easily recognizable signal words. Moreover, close inspection often reveals that it is another pattern such as description or concept/definition. Frame categories for a theme paragraph include the statement of the theme, elaboration and interpretation of the theme, and supporting information such as examples and quotes. Proposition/support paragraphs often have more than one level of ideas, such as major and minor ideas.

3. **ARGUMENTATION FOR A SINGLE THING:** These frames also provide for varying degrees of complexity. Simple arguments contain only two categories of information: the statement of a conclusion (an opinion or action) and the premises (reasons, examples, facts, quotes, etc.) that support the conclusion. More complex argumentation frames have explanations for the reasons and complex chains of reasoning as well as support for the reasons. What is critical in comprehending and composing an argument is the adequacy of the logic linking the premises to the conclusion. While this logic includes questioning the adequacy of the information in many instances, it focuses on the quality of reasoning.

4. **CONCEPT/DEFINITION FOR ONE THING:** To understand a single concept, it is important to know the following: What is the thing? What category does it belong to? What are its critical attributes? Other questions may include the following: How does it work? What does it do? What are its functions? What are examples of it? And, where appropriate, what are some nonexamples? Concept/definition paragraphs arise in literature in such works as *In Search of Excellence* by Thomas Peters and Robert Waterman and *Crime and Punishment* by Fyodor Dostoyevsky.

Texts Describing a Sequence of Something

5. **SEQUENTIAL TEXTS:** Sequential structures involve either a chronological order or a logical order, even if they are not presented in the correct order. Therefore, it is often an important task to understand or predict the correct *sequence of events*. In literature and historical texts, this may mean integrating the events in flashbacks or forecasts of events to come. In content texts, sequential texts may be *steps in a procedure* (e.g., how milk is pasteurized) or *stages in the development of something* (e.g., the stages in the life cycle of primates).

In such instances, it is important for the teacher and students to address the following categories: identify the name of the object, procedure, or initiating event; describe the stages, steps, or series, showing how one leads to another; and describe the final outcome.

6. **GOAL/ACTION/OUTCOME:** Since much of human behavior in literature or any narrative is goal oriented (e.g., winning out when one is handicapped, surviving under difficult circumstances), a useful way to summarize such behavior is to identify the goals, actions, and outcomes of the person or group. Clearly, there is a sequential component in goal/action/outcome frames, though often the goal is not revealed or implied early in the text.

Texts Containing Two or More Important Elements/Ideas

7. **COMPARE/CONTRAST TWO OR MORE THINGS:** The two elements in a compare/contrast frame are the set of similarities and the set of differences. Typically, this structure identifies what is being compared, the points that are being compared, the ways in which they are similar, and the ways in which they are different, and sometimes it provides a summary statement indicating that the things compared are more alike than different or vice versa. However, there are different ways to organize a compare/contrast structure: the whole set of similarities followed by the whole set of differences or vice versa; point-by-point comparisons of the similarities and differences; and mixes of these two patterns.

Descriptions of two or more things and discussions of two or more concepts or a concept hierarchy involve all of the categories of compare/contrast frames.

8. **PROBLEM/SOLUTION:** Most problem-solving frames pertaining to people in fiction and history focus on identifying who had the problem, the general definition of the problem, its causes and effects, the actions taken to solve the problem, and the effects of the actions. Such frames may also contain elements of decision making such as defining the available options, the resources, and the consequences of each option. Problem/solution frames for literature may focus on identifying the process of looking for solutions and the causal connection or explanation for the solution. Problem/solution frames also have a sequential component.

9. **CAUSE/EFFECT:** These frames involve establishing the effect, its cause or causes, and often an explanation linking the cause(s) to the effect. Complex cause/effect frames may involve a sequential chain of causes and/or interaction of various factors as well as multiple effects. Clearly, these frames are inherently sequential in reality, though descriptions often begin with the effects and then discuss the causes.

10. **INTERACTION FRAMES (COOPERATION AND CONFLICT):** Much of good literature involves the interaction of two or more persons or groups—e.g., the interaction of a child and an animal or a child and her/his parents. To comprehend the nature of their interaction, the key questions are these: What were the persons/groups? What were their goals? What was the nature of their interaction: conflict or cooperation? How did they act and react? (Did the interaction involve conflict or cooperation?) What was the outcome for each person/group? Interaction frames contain both sequential organization and compare/contrast organization. This pattern is present in William Golding's *Lord of the Flies* at two different levels: one level is the interaction of the main characters, and another level is the conflict between the democratic group and the totalitarian group.

34

Figure 1. Compare and Contrast Matrix Frame with Literature/Book

Of Mice and Men by John Steinbeck

Attributes	Characters	
	George	Lennie
Physical and Mental	Small man; short, thin; sharp, strong features. Common sense; smarter than Lennie.	Very large; extremely strong, but clumsy; large pale eyes. Retarded, poor memory.
Status in Life	Poor; has no job at beginning; a bum.	Poor; has no job at beginning; travels as bum with George.
Goals	Wants a job; wants to buy a small farm for himself and Lennie.	Wants small farm with George; wants to take care of rabbits.
Actions	Takes care of Lennie; acts angry at Lennie; tells Lennie what to do and how to behave; sacrifices his dreams for Lennie when he kills Lennie as the ultimate protection.	Catches mice to pet them; tries to touch soft things; does bad things unintentionally; tries to do as George says; hurts Curly; kills the puppy and Curly's wife.
Feelings	Apparent mixed feelings about Lennie but really loves him and is totally loyal; feels hope for the future until the very end.	Admires, trusts, and is totally dependent on George; likes soft things; feels he is a disappointment to George; is afraid to fight Curly; does not want to hurt anyone or anything.
What They Learned	Loyalty is more important than material things; friendship requires sacrifice.	George really loved him; did not know that George killed him.

Summary of the Book

This is the story of George and Lennie, two men who are opposite in many ways, but who are devoted friends. Lennie is retarded and extremely strong, but very gentle. He loves to touch soft things. George is small and smarter than Lennie. He takes care of his friend and protects him when Lennie's strength gets him into trouble. George also has a dream that one day they will have enough money to buy a small farm and settle down to a peaceful life.

But, as the title of the book indicates, "the best laid plans of mice and men" do not always work out. Lennie's strength gets him into trouble once again, but this time the situation is far more serious than any of their other experiences. Lennie has accidentally suffocated the wife of the owner of the farm where George and Lennie have found temporary employment. She had teased and goaded Lennie into touching her soft hair and had become afraid of Lennie's strength. Because of his own fear of again displeasing George, Lennie tries to quiet the woman by holding his hand over her mouth. But he has never learned the extent of his own strength. To save Lennie from the mob out to kill him, George kills Lennie and finally realizes his dream of a farm is gone forever.

Figure 2. Interaction Frame with Literature/Short Story

"The Dip" by Jan Andrews

Character: Tick

What were the character's goals?

> Tick wanted to have a private place where he would not have to act tough.

What were the character's actions?

> He went to the Dip to be alone.

Character: The girl

What were the character's goals?

> The girl wanted to find a place where she could be alone.

What were the character's actions?

> She found the Dip.

How did the two characters interact?

> *Conflict Interactions*
> They yelled at each other. They fought.
> *Compromise Interactions*
> They agreed that one side of the stream would belong to Tick; the other side to the girl.
> *Cooperative Interactions*
> They worked together to try to save the duck.

What were the results of the interactions for this character?

> Tick and the girl became friends. Tick learned the value of cooperation and truly shared the Dip with the girl.

What were the results of the interactions for this character?

> The girl and Tick became friends. She learned the value of cooperation; she offered to leave the Dip but stayed when she realized Tick really wanted her to stay.

Summary of the Story

The Dip was a place in the woods that Tick Merrick had found where he could be alone and be himself and not act tough. One day a girl showed up who also wanted to be alone in the Dip. For a while Tick and the girl fought with each other over the Dip. Neither wanted to leave, so finally they agreed that each could stay but on separate sides of the stream. Their dislike for each other was forgotten when they found an injured duck and tried to nurse it back to health together. The duck did not survive, but Tick and the girl had learned the value of cooperation and found they had become real friends.

36

Figure 3. Problem/Solution Frame with Content Text

The Problem

What was the problem? The Republicans threatened to take control of the national government. *Who had the problem?* The Federalists.	*What caused the problem?* The Republican party had grown stronger because— • More small farmers could vote after the voting laws were relaxed. • More people believed Republican attacks against Federalist policies.

Attempted Solutions

What actions were taken to solve the problem? The Federalists passed the Alien and Sedition Acts.

Results

What were the results of these actions? The Kentucky and Virginia resolutions supporting states' rights were written. The American People did not like the Alien and Sedition Acts. The Federalists' control of the national government was weakened.	*Was the problem solved?* No. The Federalists' attempts to solve the problem made it worse.

Content Summary

The Federalists had a problem. As the Republican party grew stronger, it threatened to take control of the national government. The Federalists attempted to solve their problem by passing the Alien and Sedition Acts. As a result of the Alien and Sedition Acts, many Americans grew angry and Federalist control of the national government was weakened. The Federalists did not solve their problem. In fact, their actions made the problem worse.

Chapter 3

STRATEGIC TEACHING AND COGNITIVE INSTRUCTION

In any framework for instruction, the role of the teacher should reflect recent research on learning, the nature of instructional materials, and instruction. In Chapter 1, we defined our framework of learning, focusing on the construction of meaning and strategic learning as the goals of instruction in the language arts. We also emphasized that the process of constructing meaning occurs in phases but is fundamentally nonlinear. Over a period of years, the model learner develops a repertoire of cognitive and metacognitive strategies which he or she employs as a means of constructing meaning.

Chapter 2 focused on defining organizational patterns that are commonly used in textual materials and in thinking generally. Model learners use this structural information to organize and analyze information in texts. Teaching students to use signal words, semantic maps, and graphic organizers has been shown to be an effective instructional strategy, especially for low-achieving students.

In this chapter, we define the concept of the *strategic teacher*, drawing on what we know from recent research on learning, organizational patterns, and instruction. Speaking generally, the strategic teacher works to develop sequences of instruction that have three broad functions: (1) they focus on constructing meaning and learning independently as the goals of learning; (2) they guide the learner through all phases of learning, recognizing that thinking is nonlinear and recursive; and (3) they teach students to use and coordinate a repertoire of both cognitive and metacognitive strategies, including knowledge of organizational patterns. Thus, in our framework, the process of instruction is essentially the mirror image of the process of learning.

The first section of this chapter defines *the role of the strategic teacher*, based on research on teaching and cognitive science. The second section describes *specific instructional strategies* that focus on teaching thinking. A third section describes briefly several *instructional approaches* that promote thinking and strategic teaching and that have been used on a large-scale basis with classroom teachers. The final section presents key concepts that characterize the instruction in these approaches. The reader must bear in mind that the research in this chapter focuses on reading and writing because there is much less research on instruction in speaking and listening that relates to strategic teaching.

THE ROLE OF THE TEACHER IN COGNITIVE INSTRUCTION

Two strands of research relate to the role of the teacher. First, *research on teaching* has yielded "thick" descriptions of and much insight into how teachers spend their time, what types of decisions they make, what constraints they face, and how effective teachers differ from less effective teachers. More recently, there has been an interest in studying the role of the teacher in student cognitive processing and expert teaching. Second, recent *research from cognitive psychology* has documented numerous instructional strategies and approaches that involve teaching students to link new information to prior knowledge, process information, solve problems, think creatively and critically across the curriculum, and make more effective decisions about their own learning.

Thus, there is an increasing merger of research interest on improving student cognitive processing in the classroom. B. F. Jones (59) refers to this emerging instruction as *cognitive instruction*, which includes instruction in all the dimensions of thinking. These include metacognition; critical and creative thinking; cognitive processes such as comprehending, composing, argumentation, inquiry, and problem solving; the various skills that are used in the service of these processes; and knowledge of content (69; see also 90 and 112). Cognitive instruction offers much to teachers, schools, and policy makers in terms of defining the goals of instruction as teaching for understanding and independent learning.

Below, we cull from both research on teaching and research on cognitive science to outline some of the key concepts in cognitive instruction that define the concept of strategic teaching. In essence, strategic teaching is cognitive instruction.

The Teacher as Manager and Executive

Current research on teaching has identified three broad definitions of the role of the teacher: as manager, as executive, and as instructor. Only the latter relates directly to cognitive instruction. However, it is useful to review the other two roles briefly because they are critical to establishing the conditions in which day-to-day cognitive instruction takes place. All too frequently the teacher as executive and manager is ignored or taken for granted in implementing cognitive instruction.

As a manager, the teacher keeps track of student records and attends to issues of time on task, discipline, and interpersonal relationships within the classroom (39, 45). As an executive, the teacher makes decisions about such things as diagnosis and prescription, the use of instructional time, the specific content to be covered, lesson plans, and homework assignments, as well as the matching of student levels of achievement to levels of text, pacing, and grouping (15, 16, 39). Both of these roles are vital to good instruction, as stated above. Yet they do not define the knowledge and behaviors for teachers as managers and executives to help students process information and construct meaning. For this we must turn to other concepts.

The Teacher as Instructor in Direct Instruction

This role has been defined differently by different researchers. For example, the Beginning Teacher Evaluation Study (BTES) model focuses on presenting the content or instructions, providing student activities, monitoring, and giving feedback (39). Other descriptions include utilizing questioning strategies (16) and communicating teacher expectations (45).

B. V. Rosenshine (91, 92) has identified teaching functions that have proved successful in experimental and correlational research on teaching: review of the previous day's work and homework, presentation of new content, guided student practice, feedback and correctives, and review of weekly and monthly work. Rosenshine refers to these teaching functions as *direct instruction* (see also 44).

The Teacher as Mediator

Other strands of research on teaching have defined a very different set of instructional functions that *mediate student cognitive processing* (110, 113). "Mediate," as used here, refers to the teacher's guiding of students through the thinking processes that are needed for constructing meaning and learning independently. Mediation also involves setting standards of excellence for learning objectives. Thus, the teacher serves as "mediator" between the task and the students. G. G. Duffy, L. R. Roehler, and G. Rackliffe (35), for example, have identified some of the ways in which effective teachers help students to construct meaning. Especially important are the teacher's skill at (1) linking new information to prior knowledge, (2) conceptualizing skills and strategies as means to learning the content and not as isolated ends in themselves, (3) focusing on information processing skills, and (4) explaining how ideas are related.

Others such as R. Feuerstein (37, 38) argue that a major difference between low- and high-achieving students is that high-achieving students have had access to mediated learning experiences, whereas low-achieving students typically have not. Much of Feuerstein's work is devoted to refining the concept of the teacher as mediator in helping students represent, interpret, and organize what they perceive.

In addition to research on student cognitive processing, D. C. Berliner (17) and others (64) have launched long-term projects to study the differences between expert and novice teachers. While this research is still in its very early stages, it is most promising because it is rich with detail about the process of day-to-day instruction. Even in the early stages, it is clear that expert teachers have developed sophisticated schemata or knowledge structures about teaching and about the content. Expert teachers also have high levels of proficiency in using these knowledge structures for such activities as planning and correcting homework assignments; linking new information and instruction to previous lessons and to the prior knowledge of the students; making sure that students understand "why"; and anticipating difficulties in learning.

The Teacher as Model for Thinking Aloud

Modeling is presented separately because of its importance in thinking. In the past, modeling has not always been defined as thinking aloud. Modeling thinking aloud is particularly important in teaching how to construct meaning (especially because of the nonlinear character of thinking), how to monitor one's own thinking, and how to answer a question through reasoning. Modeling also demonstrates how different people may construct somewhat different meanings because they have different prior knowledge and different perspectives (29, 81). Therefore, modeling is most effective when two or more persons do it in teacher/student pairs or in small groups.

SPECIFIC INSTRUCTIONAL STRATEGIES

Research from cognitive psychology has yielded an equally rich lode of findings that document the effects of specific teaching/learning strategies that mediate student thinking and independent learning. We will discuss cognitive instruction in the following areas: (1) vocabulary instruction, (2) comprehension instruction, (3) response instruction, and (4) metacognitive instruction.

Strategies for Vocabulary Instruction

According to K. Mezynski (75), only those instructional strategies that provide multiple opportunities for in-depth analysis, rich word associa-

41

tions, and extensive vocabulary use are effective. Looking up words in a dictionary and defining words in a sentence do *not* provide this "enriched" vocabulary instruction. Teaching students to brainstorm and categorize related words, discuss words in context, write stories about word meanings, construct semantic maps, and analyze the etiology of words is effective for learning vocabulary before or after focused instruction (see 14, 23, and 61 for specific strategies).

However, W. E. Nagy and P. A. Herman (77) posit that most of the thousands of words that students learn each year are learned incidentally and not through direct instruction. For this reason, they question the effectiveness of direct vocabulary instruction and emphasize teaching students to infer meaning from context. While we support this emphasis, we would provide some amount of direct instruction in vocabulary learning strategies; although the total number of words learned may be small relative to the number learned incidentally, both comprehension and composing in any subject area involve understanding key words in that area. The teacher can use effective methods of direct instruction to help assure that the students learn these key words. Direct vocabulary instruction is critical for linking new information to prior knowledge.

Strategies for Comprehension Instruction

Of the many strategies that have been documented as effective for reading and listening comprehension, the most emphasized are summarizing, representing the text graphically, using organizational patterns, and elaborating, such as constructing an analogy. (For reviews of study skill research, see 31, 54, 108, and 112.) Also, there is now a test to assess many of these strategies developed by C. E. Weinstein and V. L. Underwood (109).

A major theme that recurs throughout this literature on learning strategy instruction is that the reader's repertoire of learning strategies is modifiable through effective instruction: teachers *can* make a difference by teaching their students to use effective strategies. This is especially true for low-achieving students. However, M. C. Wittrock (113) explains why teachers sometimes do not make a difference for some or all of their students, even when they provide direct instruction. The reasons focus on the motivation and attention of the students and the teacher's ability to coordinate cognitive and metacognitive strategies.

Strategies for Response Instruction

M. Scardamalia and C. Bereiter (94) note that there is a trend away from using "processes-oriented instruction" that focuses on the process of revising and so on. Rather, they comment on four relatively new approaches to instruction found in writing research: (1) explicit strategy instruction in developing compositions, including instruction in planning and formulating goals; (2) procedural facilitation (variations of scaffolded instruction) which may vary from using word processing to providing cue cards that prompt the writer to use specific thinking processes; (3) "product-oriented instruction" emphasizing the use of organizational patterns and defining standards of style, and (4) inquiry learning in writing in which students generate rules for writing as a solution to the problem of describing or analyzing something. They discuss conferencing as the "paramount" instructional strategy for providing audience, procedural facilitation, and feedback.

We classify these strategies as *response instruction* (58). In our definition, response instruction includes any effort on the part of the teacher to help students respond meaningfully and strategically to questions in written and oral speech. Good teachers provide response instruction whenever they discuss how to write considerate texts, insist that students speak in complete sentences, and discuss how to respond to analogy problems. We believe that response instruction is a basic concept for strategic teaching and cognitive instruction.

Strategies for Metacognitive Instruction

The importance of metacognitive instruction, and more specifically of the teacher's ability to coordinate cognitive and metacognitive instruction, cannot be overestimated. S. J. Derry and D. A. Murphy (31), for example, posit that effective use of learning strategies depends on the learner's ability to make effective decisions about learning and to control the process of learning. However, a theme that emerges repeatedly in their review is that metacognitive learning strategies "cannot be trained easily or by direct instruction alone, but must be developed gradually and automated over an extended period of time." Derry and Murphy, as well as A. L. Brown (18), make a strong case for teaching students to think as they read, and discuss the implications of this approach for curriculum reform.

However, we would hasten to add that if there is one lesson to be learned in our review of research on cognitive and metacognitive strategies over the years, it is this: significant change in thinking ability will not happen without widespread application throughout the nation of the various instructional strategies and concepts that we have identified as fundamental to strategic teaching. We look forward to the new research on expert teaching for additional insight on how expert teachers achieve this coordination.

What follows in the next section are descriptions of specific programs and models that utilize a variety of these strategies developed over the years to promote strategic teaching. These are not the only approaches that embody cognitive instruction to be sure. We have selected them because they focus on cognitive and metacognitve instruction and because they provide activities that are appropriate for each phase of instruction. Equally important, we believe that each of these models is appropriate for language arts instruction. Additionally, we describe various guides and other sources that embody cognitive instruction and strategic teaching.

APPROACHES THAT PROMOTE STRATEGIC TEACHING

Specific Programs and Models

Reciprocal Teaching: This approach, developed by A. S. Palincsar and A. L. Brown (81), involves the coordination and sustained instruction of four specific strategies within the context of what the authors call *reciprocal teaching*. The four strategies are predicting, clarifying, generating questions, and summarizing. Reciprocal teaching involves scaffolded instruction, which requires the teacher and students to assume the teacher role with a gradual release of the teacher's direction so that the students ultimately take responsibility for their own learning. The teacher works actively to help students to link new information to prior knowledge, examine their own logic, and use what is learned in diverse applications. Dialogue plays a key role in this process in terms of not only teacher/student or student/student dialogue but also the self-dialogue that occurs as a teacher or student thinks aloud. Palincsar (80) has several examples of this dialogue that illustrate the difficult art of scaffolding.

Reading Across the Curriculum (RAC): This model was developed in part by H. L. Herber (49, 50) and his colleagues (1, 2). Like reciprocal teaching, it is more than the sum of the specific strategies taught; both models reflect a philosophy about learning and teaching. RAC is very robust and includes a number of specific strategies such as predicting, responding to statements that relate to the content, restructuring the content, and constructing graphic organizers, especially where there are many unfamiliar vocabulary words. Other reading in the content-area strategies focuses on generating titles, summarizing, and semantic mapping as post-learning strategies (12, 13, 112). Additionally, active and interactive teaching is fundamental to this approach (100). R. J. Tierney, J. E. Readence, and E. K. Dishner (106) describe a broad range of these strategies specifically for classroom applications.

K-W-L Group Instruction Strategy: This strategy was developed by D. S. Ogle (78). Before reading, the teacher uses brainstorming and

44

direct questioning with the students as a group to determine what they *Know* about the content from prior instruction and personal experiences. During this prereading period, the teacher works with the students to identify key categories of information (what we would call content-specific frames) that they might expect to read about in the texts. Then the teacher asks the students to reflect individually on what they *Want* to learn (questions of personal interest, based on the key categories). The students then read to answer their questions, testing the new ideas against prior knowledge and examining faulty logic and the adequacy of information. This process may lead to withholding judgment and/or assimilating new ideas. After reading, the students articulate specific ideas and strategies that they have *Learned* as well as information they still need to learn.

Informed Strategic Learning (ISL): Developed by S. G. Paris, D. R. Cross, and M. Y. Lipson (84), ISL was one of the first large-scale projects to provide direct strategy instruction and the concept of the strategic learner (85). The program is contained largely in modules of instructional materials for students to use in discussing specific metacognitive strategies. The instruction encourages the students to generate analogies so that they and their teachers have a language for thinking about and discussing thinking. Certain metacognitive decisions, for example, are in their program analogous to reading the signs on a road map. Individual lessons emphasize informing students about the strategy, modeling, applying the strategy to text, gradually fading the strategy instruction so that students increasingly initiate and apply appropriate strategies themselves, and, finally, bridging the use of the strategy to the content areas. The results of this program have been impressive.

SPaRC: This instructional procedure was developed by the authors of this book with T. H. Anderson, B. B. Armbruster, B. E. Cox, and others (59). SPaRC has three phases of instruction to guide students throughout learning. Before reading (phase 1), the students *Survey* the text features to *Predict* the content focus and organizational pattern or frame, where appropriate. During *Read* (phase 2), the students read to confirm/reject their predictions and answer specific questions as well as to monitor their comprehension. After reading (phase 3), the teacher works with the students to *Construct* meaning, with a heavy focus on brainstorming, categorizing, and summarizing. This procedure emphasizes modeling and the use of frames and graphic outlines—sometimes to activate prior knowledge, sometimes to stimulate discussion, and often to guide reading and summarizing. Although SPaRC has yet to be formally evaluated, it has been developed through extensive field testing with numerous teachers, using the materials in various types of classrooms including classrooms with low-achieving students.

45

Guides and Conceptual Frameworks

In addition to the specific programs and models identified above that reflect the best of research on teaching and thinking, several state departments of education and professional organizations have prepared guides that adapt this research for dissemination in schools and institutions of teacher education. Virtually all of these guides were developed by researchers or in consultation with researchers. Of particular interest to the readers of this book are the documents that embody the new definition of reading. Specifically, there are the *Model Curriculum Standards: Grades Nine Through Twelve*, "English/Language Arts" (22) adopted by the California State Board of Education and guides published by the Wisconsin Department of Public Instruction (111), the Michigan Reading Association and the Michigan Department of Education (76), and the Orange County Public Schools (79).

Noteworthy also are the National Education Association monographs on thinking, the various films and instructional materials on thinking and reading published by the Association for Supervision and Curriculum Development, and the Research Within Reach series on various subject matter topics developed by the Appalachia Educational Laboratory.

KEY CONCEPTS IN COGNITIVE INSTRUCTION AND STRATEGIC TEACHING

In addition to specifying the various instructional strategies and approaches discussed above, research on thinking has generated a number of key concepts that should be central to strategic teaching and cognitive instruction. We address these in the next section.

Direct Instruction Redefined

An interesting result of the research on thinking is the redefining of direct instruction. That is, S. G. Paris, D. R. Cross, and M. Y. Lipson (84), and others (43, 96) have argued that in training students to use specific strategies, it is imperative to provide explicit strategy instruction. Specifically, they discuss the need to inform students of exactly what the strategy is, how it works, why it should be used, and where and when to use it. No doubt most teachers will recognize that this is "the 5 W's plus How" in strategy instruction: who, what, where, when, why, and how. Additionally, research on thinking conceptualizes instruction in strategies and skills as a means to understanding the content. Thus, in contrast to the definition of direct instruction given in research on teaching, the definition of direct instruction given in metacognitive and cognitive research generally refers to explicit strategy instruction.

Misconceptions

This concept comes largely from research in science, but it is a powerful concept and one that we predict will be a key concept in other areas of strategic teaching. C. W. Anderson and L. Smith (3) and K. J. Roth (93) have studied the teaching of science to middle grade students for several years. Apparently, a major problem in student achievement in science is that most learners hold very tenacious misconceptions about how the world works. These misconceptions are so strong that they essentially prevent conceptual change from taking place. Even high-achieving students, for example, can master tests on such concepts as photosynthesis and motion, and still not really comprehend that plants make their own food through the process of photosynthesis and that objects do not acquire motion when thrown.

According to these and other researchers, these misconceptions persist largely because (1) they are meaningful to students, and (2) the instruction allows students to regurgitate information in multiple-choice questions without any real learning. The *only* instructional strategy that facilitates conceptual change is to confront the misconception directly throughout the instruction: ask students to give their own explanations before focused instruction, provide very explicit teacher explanation or textual materials that require students to understand the correct explanation during focused instruction, and then compare the new conception to the old misconception to render it meaningless after focused instruction. Thus, the concept of direct instruction takes on yet another meaning—specifically the need to articulate directly what ideas have changed.

Scaffolded Instruction and the Concept of Apprenticeship

A. Collins and J. S. Brown (25) have analyzed several "success models" that exemplify excellence in teaching, including reciprocal teaching in reading and the methods of teaching writing developed by M. Scardamalia and C. Bereiter (95). The "hallmark" stategies that were critical in these approaches were (1) modeling, especially thinking aloud about how to apply the strategy or skill; (2) coaching, which involves diagnosing problems, prescribing correctives, and providing feedback; (3) inquiry; (4) articulation (getting students to articulate their knowledge and thinking processes); (5) reflection about the process of thinking; and (6) exploration (pushing students to extend their learning).

Equally important, Collins and Brown define three *principles of sequencing instruction* that they think are critical for good teaching: scaf-

folding, increasing complexity, and increasing diversity. In their definition, scaffolding refers to the support the teacher gives to students by
carrying out some part of the task initially until they can progress without these supports. These supports may be cues such as providing frame
categories and questions, teacher explanations, changing misconceptions,
coaching, and the like. However, fading or gradually removing these
supports is essential if students are to become independent learners.
Increasing complexity and increasing diversity refer to both the content
and the task. We will return to these principles of sequencing in Chapter 5 where we define principles of sequencing for "enriched" skills
instruction.

Their concept of apprenticeship includes the six instructional strategies
and the three principles of sequencing. However, their notion of apprenticeship is, above all, the craft of teaching the subtle nuances of constructing meaning and solving problems, the expertise of making good
decisions about what is important to learn and how to learn it, as well as
both critical and creative thinking about the content. Apprenticeship is,
in essence, the coordination of cognitive and metacognitive processes
that arises from years of expert teaching in a given area.

Finally, we would like to emphasize a point that Collins and Brown
made, but did not identify as a specific strategy like modeling. The
instruction in each of their success models, either implicitly or explicitly,
raises and confronts misconceptions about what it is that the model
learner does. That is, Scardamalia and Bereiter, for example, note that
children perceive of writing as "knowledge telling": they write what
they know with little reference to planning, revising, or other thinking
processes. One reason why Scardamalia and Bereiter's methods work so
well is that they confront this misconception directly.

Given how tenacious misconceptions are, future research and future
instruction may discover that misconceptions about reading, writing,
listening, and speaking, and about themselves as learners, are at the core
of poor and average achievement. If this is true, studying and confront-
ing these misconceptions directly may prove to be a powerful instructional strategy that attacks the very roots of learning problems.

The Phases of Instruction

Noting that the model reader engages in different cognitive activities
before, during, and after focused learning, T. H. Anderson (6) argues
that instruction should address each phase of learning. R. E. Mayer (70)
labels these phases of learning and instruction selection, organization,
and integration respectively. He shows how the teacher can help students
to use various features of the instructional materials such as objectives,

reviews, and summaries as aids to selecting, organizing, and integrating information.

These arguments have influenced much of our thinking, and they are obviously key concepts in this book. What we argue here and elsewhere (56) is that teachers can sequence instruction in terms of each phase of learning. That is, teachers can select and sequence specific teaching/learning strategies for preparatory learning, for on-line processing during the instruction focused on the objective, and for consolidating/extending the learning after focused instruction. At this point, we return to the notion stated at the beginning of the chapter—namely, that the strategic teacher's repertoire of instructional strategies should in part be the mirror image of the repertoire of thinking strategies used by the strategic learner. Further, it is not surprising that the research on instruction reviewed above reflects many parallels to research on learning in the same areas—though it is surprising that neither teachers nor researchers make explicit reference to this useful organizing concept.

Thus, instructional strategies *before focused instruction* might emphasize discussing the task; selecting important features of the text; and activating prior knowledge of the content, organizational patterns, and thinking strategies, as well as setting specific learning goals. Strategies *during focused instruction* would emphasize monitoring comprehension/composing and on-line processing for text segments. Clarifying and modifying ideas, summarizing, elaborating, and taking notes are research-based strategies that would be appropriate during focused instruction. Strategies *after focused instruction* would emphasize constructing meaning for the passage as a whole, assessing achievement of learning (articulation), and extending learning by application to a diversity of new situations.

A fundamental element of the learning process within each phase, thinking is recursive and nonlinear. It was most surprising to us to note that we found little explicit mention of *recursive and nonlinear instruction* in the literature on instruction discussed above and in Chapter 2. Perhaps one reason for this is that most of the research on instruction is on specific strategies that do not span all the phases of learning.

At the same time, the notion that instruction is recursive and nonlinear is strongly implied or referred to indirectly in the various references to helping students to link new information to prior knowledge, rethink and revise ideas, modify predictions, clarify, change misconceptions, question earlier thoughts, and summarize. All these thinking activities require behavior on the part of the teacher that is inherently nonlinear and recursive. Thus, although the notion of nonlinear and recursive instruction is largely implicit, it is nevertheless present in research on instruction in the language arts and content areas, and we would include

49

it as an element of strategic teaching.

Planning Guide 3, located at the end of this chapter, provides a summary of the various instructional strategies that are appropriate for before, during, and after focused instruction. The labels within each phase identify the specific instructional strategies that are critical to the concept of strategic teaching. This list, culled from the research on instruction in Chapter 2 and in this chapter, includes a coordination of cognitive and metacognitive instructional strategies.

Comments on how to use this guide to sequence content and skills instruction in a given learning situation are offered in the introduction to Part 2. It is crucial to note that a single learning situation would *not* use all of these strategies. Thus, this guide is intended to serve as a summary and review of key instructional strategies from which a teacher might select specific ones for each phase of learning.

To review, this chapter identified four dimensions of strategic teaching. First, we discussed four elements of the role of teacher in strategic teaching: the teacher as manager and executive, making decisions about pacing, content, diagnosis, and prescription; the teacher as instructor in direct instruction; the teacher as mediator in student cognitive processing; and the teacher as model in thinking aloud about constructing meaning and strategic learning. Second, we discussed specific instructional strategies that mediate thinking in four categories: vocabulary, comprehension, composition (which we called *response instruction*), and metacognition. Third, we described briefly a number of specific programs and guides that have integrated instructional strategies from the various categories into a cohesive program or approach that provides instruction throughout the phases of learning. Fourth, we identified key concepts in cognitive instruction and strategic teaching: the new definition of direct instruction as explicit strategy instruction, misconceptions, the concepts of scaffolded instruction and apprenticeship, and, finally, the phases of instruction that parallel the phases of learning and provide instruction for recursive and nonlinear thinking.

Planning Guide 3

Thinking Processes and Instructional Strategies in the Language Arts*

Thinking Processes	Instructional Strategies
PREPARATORY PROCESSING	**BEFORE FOCUSED INSTRUCTION**
Comprehend objective/task	*Discuss objective/task*
Define learning objectives	Discuss/Define nature of task
Consider task/audience	Discuss audience/learning goals
Determine criteria for success	Model/Elicit criteria for success
Preview/Select materials/cues at hand	*Preview/Select materials/cues at hand*
Skim features and graphic aids	Model/Guide previewing of materials
Determine content focus/organizational pattern	Elicit content focus/organizational pattern
Activate prior knowledge	*Activate/Provide background knowledge*
Access content and vocabulary	Elicit/Provide content and vocabulary
Access categories and structure	Confront misconceptions, discuss strategies
Access strategies/plans	Elicit/Provide categories and structural pattern
Focus interest/Set purpose	*Focus interest/Set purpose*
Form hypotheses and questions/Make predictions	Brainstorm, model/guide hypotheses and predictions
Represent/Organize ideas (Categorize/Outline)	Model/Guide formulating questions for meaning
ON-LINE PROCESSING (Text Segments)	**DURING FOCUSED INSTRUCTION**
Modify hypotheses/Clarify ideas	*Pause and reflect/Discuss (after segments)*
Check hypotheses, predictions, questions	Model/Guide checking predictions, etc.
Compare to prior knowledge	Model/Guide comparing to prior knowledge
Ask clarification questions	Model/Guide asking clarification questions
Examine logic of argument, flow of ideas	Elicit/Discuss faulty logic/contradictions/gaps
Generate new questions	Model/Guide raising issues/formulation questions
Integrate ideas	*Integrate ideas (after segments)*
Select important concepts/words	Brainstorm, model/guide reasoning for selection
Connect and organize ideas, summarize	Model/Guide summarizing text segments
Assimilate new ideas	*Assimilate new ideas (after segments)*
Articulate changes in knowledge	Brainstorm, model/guide articulation process
Evaluate ideas/products	Provide conferences/feedback, correctives
Withhold judgment	Discuss reasons for withholding judgment

*Adapted from *Teaching Reading as Thinking* (82). Reprinted with permission.

Planning Guide 3—*Continued*

Thinking Processes and Instructional Strategies in the Language Arts

Thinking Processes	Instructional Strategies
CONSOLIDATING/EXTENDING ("The Big Picture")	**AFTER FOCUSED INSTRUCTION**
Integrate/Organize meaning for whole	*Integrate/Organize meaning for whole*
Categorize and integrate information, conclude	Brainstorm key ideas, find categories/patterns
Summarize key ideas and connections	Discuss organizational patterns/standards
Evaluate/Revise/Edit	Model/Guide return to standards/evaluation process
Assess achievement of purpose/learning	*Assess achievement of purpose*
Compare new learnings to prior knowledge	Discuss "old" misconceptions/new learnings
Identify gaps in learning and information	Guide identification, diagnose/prescribe, coach
Generate new questions/next steps	Provide opportunities for questions and followup
Extend learning	*Extend learning*
Translate/Apply to new situations	Increase complexity/diversity of content and task
Rehearse and study	Discuss/Guide mnemonics and in-depth study skills

In Part 2, we present five examples for teaching specific content and skills objectives. These examples can be used as models for sequencing instruction for both language arts and content area objectives. Each of the examples was developed from the Planning Guides in Part 1. Therefore, these examples embody the guidelines regarding learning, organizational patterns, and instruction given earlier. The instruction in each example is organized in terms of the concept of an *instructional sequence*, devised to address each of the phases in a learning situation (before, during, and after focused learning). Therefore, each instructional sequence has three distinct phases: before focused instruction, during focused instruction, and after focused instruction.

We use the phrase "sequence of instruction" because our examples are not traditional lesson plans. That is, each example illustrates a sequence of instructional activities and provides key information, such as questions, graphic outline structures, and models that would be needed to teach a specific objective. The sequences provide opportunities for activating prior knowledge, thinking aloud, reflecting, revising, graphic outlining, and summarizing for each objective.

CONTENT-DRIVEN AND SKILLS-DRIVEN INSTRUCTION

The examples in this section are intended to illustrate not only the sequence of instruction but also the interaction of the teacher and students necessary to achieve content and skills objectives. Content objectives may be fairly specific, such as understanding the meaning of the symbols in a specific poem or a comparison of two poems. In all three of the content examples in Chapter 4, the selection of specific skills, such as writing a theme paragraph and compare/contrast analysis, is *content-driven*. That is, they are selected for a given sequence of instruction because they are needed to understand the content. Thus, in content-driven instruction, specific skills are conceptualized as means to an end, not as ends in themselves.

Content-driven instruction contrasts with *skills-driven instruction*, in which the objective focuses on a specific skill such as summarizing. Good skills instruction includes (1) explicit instruction about the skill itself and how to use it as a *strategy* to understand the meaning in particular instruction, (2) scaffolded instruction with adequate opportunities to apply the skill using diverse organizational patterns and increasing complexity of the content, and (3) coordination of both cognitive and metacognitive processes. There are two examples of instruction seeking to teach skills as strategies in Chapter 5.

ORGANIZATION OF CHAPTERS 4 AND 5

Within these five examples, there is some diversity with respect to genre and grade level. Clearly, the first example in Chapter 4, focusing on *The Pigman*, is not appropriate for most elementary students; yet the sequence of instruction within it is appropriate for reading novels and short stories at many grade levels. The second example on rocks is typical of science passages in basal readers and in science texts for upper elementary students, but this example may be used as a model of instruction for any compare/contrast text. The content and the instruction on poetry in the third content example are appropriate for various grade levels from middle elementary through middle high school. It is an introductory sequence assuming little prior knowledge.

In Chapter 5, the first skills example deals with finding main ideas and is most appropriate for middle elementary school students. It may, however, be useful for any student lacking this skill. This sequence assumes that students have some background knowledge of signal words and organizational patterns. However, we have provided information on both topics in case background knowledge is lacking. The second example in Chapter 5 is intended to serve as an introduction to argumentation at various grade levels from middle elementary school throughout high school.

INDIVIDUAL DIFFERENCES IN CLASSROOM SITUATIONS

There will be occasions when we have specified a review that it may be necessary to provide information. At other times we may provide information that the students already know. This is to be expected when one presents generic examples. What is important is to understand the flow or sequence of information, whether it is review information or new information. Additionally, it is critical to understand the interweaving of both cognitive and metacognitive strategies as well as reading, writing, listening, and speaking.

A Cautionary Note: We have made no attempt to estimate how long each example will take to teach. This will depend entirely on other factors, including the prior knowledge, interests, and ability levels of the students, the teacher's pacing of the class, the difficulty of the materials used, the number of variations used, and the amount of time allotted for each lesson period. *When the instruction lasts more than a day or so, it is crucial to begin each succeeding day by reviewing the previous day's activities and relating them to the new instruction.*

INSTRUCTIONAL DESIGN AS A THINKING PROCESS

We began with the following assumptions about the nature of the task for each objective: (1) the learner would need some instructional activities for each phase of learning, (2) the learner would need to learn or review information about organizational patterns, (3) the sequence of instruction would need to address all three phases of thinking as well as refer to structural information, and (4) we would have to coordinate the use of the three Planning Guides and the content to craft each sequence of instruction. To recall, the three Planning Guides are—

- Planning Guide 1—Thinking Processes in the Language Arts
- Planning Guide 2—Frames for Generic Organizational Patterns
- Planning Guide 3—Thinking Processes and Instructional Strategies in the Language Arts.

We began the planning process by selecting the key concepts and structural information to be taught for in-depth comprehension. Then we looked at Planning Guide 1 to review the phases of learning, focusing particularly on assessing the prior knowledge of the students. Next, we used Planning Guide 3 to review key instructional strategies for each learning phase. Then we returned to Resource Guide 1 and used the empty spaces in it to outline what we thought was a workable sequence of instruction for each learning phase. This outlining process and the period of sustained designing involved integrating information from both of the other Planning Guides. It also involved coordinating meta-cognitive and cognitive processes as well as integrating reading, writing, listening, and speaking.

Essentially, we treated the process of designing instruction as a thinking process. Before sustained efforts to compose the sequence, we began by "skimming" the objective for cues about meaning and structural information. Then we reviewed each guide to activate prior knowledge and set instructional goals. The outline we constructed to represent our ideas was treated essentially as a hypothesis, knowing that we would modify and refine it as we generated the first draft of instruction.

The process of drafting/designing during the on-line processing phase was very much a start-and-pause process. It involved recurring cycles of drafting a segment of instruction and pausing for reflection—sometimes to test it against prior knowledge, sometimes to evaluate it against our instructional goals, sometimes to clarify some question about the meaning of the content or the use of organizational patterns, and sometimes to verify the wording of a quote or other information. Naturally this process resulted in revisions to each segment of the design as well as to our understanding of the content and the structural pattern.

After drafting the various segments, we paused again to consolidate our conception by trying to see how the various segments fitted together in "the big picture" and to assess the extent to which the design as a whole met our objectives. We revised different aspects of it to make the different components more cohesive. Then we did what other good writers do: we extended our learning by "conferencing" with others to view our product from different perspectives. Following this conferencing, we eliminated one of our examples, rewrote portions of other examples, and made numerous word-level and sentence-level changes.

Not surprisingly, given this level of in-depth processing, none of our current examples matches the original outline, or follows exactly the order of instructional strategies in Planning Guide 3. These guides were not created to be followed exactly. They are, as their name implies, only guides for reviewing and organizing thinking about the sequence of instruction in general terms. It is inevitable that the process of applying the guides to specific objectives will yield unique variations and modifications which reflect the interests and habits of the designer as well as the characteristics of the students.

Chapter 4

CONTENT OBJECTIVES

OVERVIEW

The three examples in this chapter have been selected to provide a diversity of instructional problems, genres, and organizational patterns. We began thinking about these sequences with the three Planning Guides in mind. Our central task was to provide instruction that would focus on meaning and the nonlinear quality of thinking as well as address the three phases of instruction (preparation, on-line processing, and consolidation) and the coordination of cognitive and metacognitive processes.

Example 1 (Literature / Novel)

The first example focuses on the development of a theme essay for *The Pigman*. We thought that many adolescents might have misconceptions about the differences between adolescence and old age. We also assumed that many students may have poorly conceived notions about the categories of information that are appropriate for a theme. Therefore, the first phase of instruction focuses on eliciting prior knowledge about age roles and the concept of a theme essay. A skillful teacher will use the frame questions in Figure 1a (or her or his own questions) to structure the discussion, building on existing ideas so that the students have some "ownership" of the criteria that are generated for the essay.

The focal point of this sequence, however, is the spider map in Figure 1c. We generated the instruction and the theme essay from this map. Notice how the parallel structure of the lines on either side of the theme statement in the map reflects the parallel subthemes or minor ideas about the characters. Writing a theme essay is a very effective means of conceptualizing such relationships and consolidating learning. However, assessment of learning after focused instruction is critical in this case because it is important to relate the new learnings back to any misconceptions about adolescence and old age and to consolidate the students' understanding of a theme essay.

Example 2 (Content Passage/Science)

We chose the second example to illustrate two problems that occur frequently. First, vocabulary is a major problem in science and other content texts. Therefore, the instruction should provide opportunities (1) to clarify students' understanding of specific terms and (2) to examine the relationship of the ideas in depth later through questioning. Second, many students lack strategies for organizing and integrating the information in comparative organizational patterns, especially when the content is technical or abstract. Matrices are the most appropriate graphic for outlining comparative information; they facilitate compare/contrast analysis because the matrix structure reflects how one set of information (the columns) systematically cuts across the second set of information (the rows).

Most of the instruction in Example 2 is built around a matrix with the three types of rocks as column headings and the key points of comparison as row headings. The first activities focus on constructing the matrix. Then, once the information is in the matrix, there are several analytical activities. First, there is a compare/contrast analysis that yields the type of information that students would be required to comprehend and remember. Second, the students use the matrix to generate hypotheses about the relationship of items in the matrix; these hypotheses would then be the topic of subsequent research. Third, the students may complete assignments that relate the subject matter, rocks, to broader issues in various content areas. Finally, the last extension activity discusses how to use the matrices for other topics.

It is also useful to reiterate how important this mapping/graphic procedure is for planning sequences of instruction. Once we mapped the information from the science text into the matrix, we saw that there were few obvious similarities among the rocks. The types of rock were far more different then they were similar. At the same time, the matrix format permitted us to see relationships that would have been difficult to infer from the prose text. Our questions were generated from this analysis. Had the analysis of the matrix revealed more similarities or overall patterns, as is often the case, we would have used the matrix for writing an essay as well.

Example 3 (Literature/Poetry)

For the sequence of instruction on the Wordsworth poems in Example 3, our goal was to help the students appreciate Wordsworth's view of the world as expressed through figurative language, the vividness and flow of the language, and the nuances of meaning. To attain this level of understanding requires the coordination of many cognitive and metacognitive processes as well as considerable prior knowledge about poetry as a genre, types of figurative language, and other elements of style.

Yet, many students have little background knowledge about the style of specific poets, the "sound" of a poem as it might be read by a model reader of poetry, the thinking processes involved in constructing meaning for poetic language, or the notion of thinking about nature and the world. Consequently, this instruction focuses on modeling (1) an oral reading, (2) the cognitive and metacognitive processes needed to construct meaning for one poem, and (3) the differences in meaning and perspective that are attained from several "passes" at reading the same poem and from considering different points of view as the students take turns at thinking aloud. In a real classroom situation, we would also have had a strong focus on comparing and contrasting the poems.

CONTENT EXAMPLE 1

Content Objective (Literature: Short Story or Novel)

Students will read *The Pigman* by Paul Zindel to understand how stages of development are states of mind as well as physical stages.

Overview of Instructional Strategies

Before Focused Instruction: The teacher elicits students' prior knowledge of stages of development and provides/reviews background information of categories for determining theme, strategies, and information about genre.

During Focused Instruction: Students refine the hypotheses they formulated earlier.

After Focused Instruction: Students write about the theme.

BEFORE FOCUSED INSTRUCTION

► *Discuss Objective/Task*

EXPLAIN that the purpose of this instruction is to consider major themes about adolescence and old age in *The Pigman*.[1]

► *Activate/Provide Prior Knowledge*

ASK students to define one characteristic of adolescence and one of old age, and then evaluate whether or not the characteristic is unique to adolescence or old age.

At the end of the discussion, REVIEW the unique characteristics of each period of life.[2]

► *Preview Materials at Hand*

If necessary, REVIEW/EXPLAIN briefly questions in Figure 1a. Students may use these questions to help identify the theme.

---

[1]**Variation:** Elicit characteristics of novels: many episodes, extensive character development, complicated interactions among characters, extensive description of characters' actions and feelings, setting described in detail, more than one theme. The unity of a novel derives from its plot.

Discuss the usefulness of understanding these characteristics: to appreciate and comprehend the structure of a novel; to appreciate this form of communication; to approach a new novel with expectations of its form; to compare and contrast one novel with another.

[2]**Variation:** Summarize the characteristics of adolescence and old age in a matrix on the chalkboard. Possible row headings for the matrix are Work, School, Personal Relationships, Responsibilities, and Physical Characteristics.

EXPLAIN/ELICIT that Zindel focuses on different roles in adolescence and old age, and that many of the clues for the theme come from the behavior of the characters as they move from one role to another.

Figure 1a. Theme Frame

---

1. Are there any clues to the theme in the title?
2. Does the author state the theme(s) directly?
3. What topic does the author give the most attention to? (surviving, hardships, search for meaning, etc.)
4. Are there clues from the characters' conversations or thoughts?
5. How do the characters change? What lessons do they learn?
6. What are the main problems or conflicts? (one character against another, etc.)
7. Are there clues to the theme from the characters' actions? Is their behavior normal or deviant? Rational or irrational? Constructive or destructive?
8. Is there anything about the setting that is distinctive or unusual?
9. What additional themes are discovered in outside bibliographies—e.g., teacher's notes, literary criticisms?

► *Focus Interest/Set Purpose*

EXPLAIN that it is helpful to generate a general hypothesis of a theme and then to look for concrete examples to refine the hypothesis.[3]

MODEL how to form a general hypothesis of a theme and a rationale for it by thinking aloud or ask a student to model the process.

DURING FOCUSED INSTRUCTION

► *Clarify Ideas/Construct Meaning for Segments*

DISCUSS students' general impressions of Zindel's theme about development and the different age roles in life. ASK each student to give a rationale or support for his/her ideas.

GUIDE students to relate specific examples to the theme. For example, ASK students to think about the meaning of the adolescents' dressing up in adult clothes and playing adult roles: were they being childlike or more adult? Then DISCUSS how this episode relates to students' general impressions of the theme.

---

[3]**Variation:** To help students make predictions about the theme, give them an opinionnaire with theme statements such as:

1. I think everyone should act his/her age.
2. I think it is all right for older people to pretend they are young.

► *Clarify Ideas*

During or after the discussion about themes, ASK students to pause and identify anything they do not understand.[4]

DISCUSS the value of looking back to reread or skim certain portions of the novel to help clarify misunderstandings.

AFTER FOCUSED INSTRUCTION

► *Construct Meaning for the Whole Passage*

Using the questions in Figure 1b as a model, ASK students to suggest and discuss criteria for writing about a theme.

Figure 1b. Questions for Writing about Themes

---

1.   What is the theme of the selection? (Give a general statement.)
2.   Can I be more specific? Can I elaborate?
3.   What are some key examples of the author's illustration of the theme—e.g., the characters' behavior?
4.   What does this theme mean for my life? For other people's lives?

ASK students to use the criteria to write a summary of the theme.[5] A sample summary follows.

---

[4]**Variation:** Have students compare their ideas about the theme to ideas in other sources such as teacher's notes and literary critiques.

[5]**Variation:** Guide students to outline the theme and key examples in a spider map (see Figure 1c) using the questions in Figure 1b to help construct the map. Have students write an essay using the map to organize the text.

Sample Summary of a Theme

One of the main themes in *The Pigman* by Paul Zindel is that people should act their age. People who do not can get into a lot of trouble and hurt many people.

In this book, the characters constantly shift in and out of different age roles. Lorraine and John are teenagers. Most teenagers spend their time in school with other teenagers, but Lorraine and John are bored in school. As a way to overcome their boredom, they befriend an old man, Mr. Pignatti whom they call Pigman, and spend increasing amounts of time with him in his house. Most of the episodes in the book tell how John, Lorraine, and the Pigman try desperately to have fun.

The problem is not that the three characters are friends but that they are trying to return to the easy life and pleasures of childhood. For example, John and Lorraine dress up in clothes that belonged to Mr. Pignatti's wife and pretend that they are adults, just as many young children do. Mr. Pignatti buys John and Lorraine and himself many gifts; most of them are toys such as roller skates. For a long time Mr. Pignatti does not tell his young friends that his wife is dead; he even seems to have trouble admitting it to himself. Even the nickname John and Lorraine have given Mr. Pignatti—Pigman—indicates their childish behavior. Thus, what the characters want and the ways they behave are in conflict with the responsibilities and realities of being an adolescent and an older, retired man.

There are three episodes that show the theme very clearly. First, all three characters roller skate inside Mr. Pignatti's house. When Mr. Pignatti tries to climb the stairs with his skates on, he falls and has a heart attack. Second, while Mr. Pignatti is in the hospital, John and Lorraine invite all their friends to Mr. Pignatti's house for a party. The party gets out of hand, and the teenagers make a terrible mess of the house. Mr. Pignatti comes home while all of this is going on and seems to begin to realize the danger of trying to act like an irresponsible child again. Finally, John and Lorraine arrange to meet Mr. Pignatti at the zoo. While they are there, Mr. Pignatti has another heart attack and dies. Lorraine blames herself and John for his death, but John has learned that not only were they at fault, but Mr. Pignatti was, too. All three were behaving in ways that were inappropriate for their ages.

In our society, many adults yearn to be young and foolishly try to behave like children; also, many teenagers resent not being treated as adults and, in contrast, sometimes behave very childishly. This novel shows in a very effective and moving way that although having friends of different ages may be a good thing, it is important to accept the age that you are and behave accordingly.

▶ *Assess Achievement of Purpose/Learning*

DISCUSS what students have learned about the roles of various developmental stages in life, especially adolescence and old age. COMPARE their ideas to ideas they had before the lesson. RELATE these new learnings to personal growth/experience.

▶ *Extend Learning*

DISCUSS other authors who write about similar themes and/or other works by Paul Zindel to generate interest in further reading.

DISCUSS other opportunities to use the theme frame—e.g., for interpreting themes in other genres.

Figure 1c. Spider Map

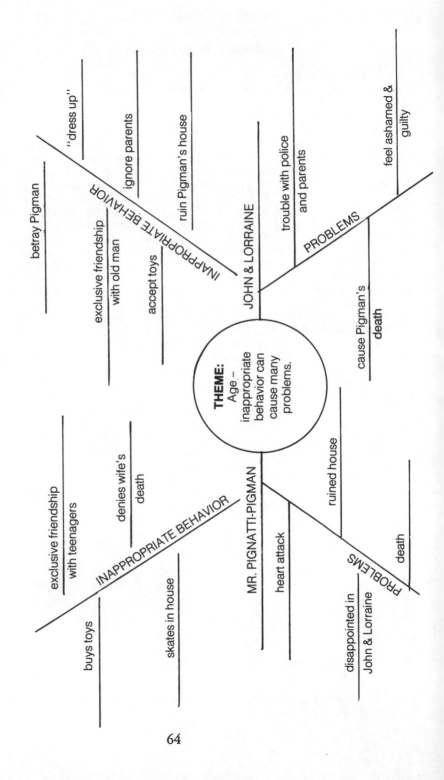

THEME:
Age – inappropriate behavior can cause many problems.

INAPPROPRIATE BEHAVIOR

JOHN & LORRAINE

betray Pigman

"dress up"

ignore parents

ruin Pigman's house

exclusive friendship with old man

accept toys

PROBLEMS

trouble with police and parents

feel ashamed & guilty

cause Pigman's **death**

INAPPROPRIATE BEHAVIOR

MR. PIGNATTI-PIGMAN

exclusive friendship with teenagers

denies wife's death

buys toys

skates in house

heart attack

ruined house

PROBLEMS

disappointed in John & Lorraine

death

64

CONTENT EXAMPLE 2

Content Objective (Content Area Passage/Rocks)

The students read a text to learn about the three types of rocks.

Overview of Instructional Strategies

Before Focused Instruction: The students predict the content of the passage from prior knowledge of rocks and a survey of text features.

During Focused Instruction: The students read to construct a matrix.

After Focused Instruction: The class constructs and analyzes the matrix to make compare/contrast statements.

BEFORE FOCUSED INSTRUCTION

▶ *Discuss Objective/Task*

EXPLAIN that students will read a text and construct a matrix to learn about rocks. LINK this objective to previous instruction.

Ask the students why it is important to know about rocks. DISCUSS the various occupations in modern society that need to know about rocks.[1]

▶ *Activate Prior Knowledge*

ELICIT what the students already know about rocks:
1. What are some examples of rocks? (coal, marble, slate, etc.)
2. Where do rocks come from? (Some are found on the earth's surface, some below it, and some on the floors of oceans, seas, and lakes.)
3. How are rocks formed? (They are built up from minerals that harden like the stalactites and stalagmites in caves, from the pressure of the earth's layers on top of one another, and from molten lava that cools and becomes rock.)

EXPLAIN that the class will read the text to compare their answers with those of the author.

▶ *Focus Interest/Set Purpose*

ASK the students to *skim* the title, subtitles, and graphics.

---

[1]**Variation:** DISCUSS uses of rocks in earlier historic eras—e.g., for cavedwellers.

With the students, PREDICT the text structure (compare and contrast because the text discusses three types of rocks) and the main categories of information to be discussed.

As a way of summarizing the discussion, LIST the three types of rocks (igneous, sedimentary, and metamorphic) on the chalkboard. LIST also the key categories of discussion—e.g., characteristics of rocks and the process of forming rocks.

▶ *Discuss Objective/Task*

EXPLAIN the following:
1. There will be a number of difficult vocabulary words.
2. Textbooks have different ways of providing definitions of difficult words in the body of the text.

DISCUSS/REVIEW the various clues for finding definitions in the text:
1. In parentheses after the word
2. In between commas after the word
3. After "that is"
4. In a sentence after the word.[2]

DURING FOCUSED INSTRUCTION

▶ *Construct Meaning for Segments*

USE start/stop procedures to read and process segments of text. For example, ASK students to *read* the text for one type of rock. Then stop to *select* important information and assimilate new ideas. (Use other stopping points if the text is organized differently.)

▶ *Clarify Ideas*

PROVIDE opportunities during this start/stop process for students—
1. To *clarify* or *identify* vocabulary problems and gaps of information.
2. To *ask questions* about the meaning and the importance of specific segments of the text or specific categories of information. (This is particularly important in reading difficult texts.)

---

[2]**Variation:** It may be appropriate for the students to figure out the meaning of difficult words before they read. ASK the students to (1) *skim* the text again to *list* all vocabulary, (2) *infer* their meanings from the sentences around each word and *write* their definitions out before reading, and (3) *infer* the categories for each word—e.g., compacting is a process that forms rocks. Use a glossary or dictionary to check meanings if necessary.

► *Construct Meaning for the Whole Passage*

CONSTRUCT a matrix on the chalkboard such as the one in Figure 2a and fill it in as a class.

Figure 2a. Rock Matrix

	Igneous		Sedimentary			Metamorphic
	Extrusive	Intrusive	Clastic	Chemical	Organic	
Formation Processes	Cooling Hardening		Compacting Cementing	Evaporation Precipitation	Hardening Compacting	Heat Pressure
Materials Used in the Formation	Magma (molten rock)		Small pieces of rock	Minerals	Organic matter such as shells and plants	Existing rock
Location of the Formation Processes	On the earth's surface	Below the earth's surface	Ocean floors On the earth's surface			12 – 16 kilometers below the surface
Examples	Obsidian Perlite Pumice	Granite	Bracia Sandstone Shale	Limestone Rock salt Rock gypsum	Coal Chalk Coquina	Gneiss Marble Quartzite

EXPLAIN that these general categories of information (the column and row headings) are likely to be used to organize information about rocks.

EXPLAIN that the columns summarize the important information for each type of rock and that the rows encourage a compare/contrast analysis across categories.

ANALYZE the matrix for similarities and differences. Figure 2b shows some compare/contrast statements that can be made.

Figure 2b. Compare/Contrast Statements
About the Three Types of Rocks

1. There are no similarities among the three kinds of rocks.
2. Similarities between *igneous and sedimentray rock* are as follows:
    a. They both have subtypes:
        *   Igneous rock can be extrusive or intrusive, depending on where it is formed;
        *   Sedimentary rock has three subtypes—clastic, chemical, and organic—which differ in terms of how they are formed and what they are formed from.
    b. Igneous and some organic sedimentary rock are formed by hardening.
    c. Igneous and clastic sedimentary rock are formed from rock.
    d. Sedimentary and extrusive igneous rock are formed on the earth's surface.
3. Similarities between *igneous and metamorphic rock* are as follows:
    a. Both are formed from rock.
    b. Metamorphic and intrusive igneous rock are formed below the earth's surface.
4. *Sedimentary and metamorphic* rock are similar in that clastic sedimentary and metamorphic rock are formed from rock.

► *Assess Achievement of Purpose/Learning*

DISCUSS what has been learned and what pieces of information are missing.

► *Extend Learning*

GENERATE new questions for learning with the students that use the information in the matrix. EXPLAIN that the students are to integrate information in the different cells of the matrix to generate hypotheses about the answers.

ASK the students to identify the rows containing information for the answers. These hypotheses may then be verified by the teacher or subsequent research.
1. Granite, marble, and quartzite are very hard. Why? (These rocks are found [or formed] beneath the earth's surface where the pressure is very great. Rows 1, 3, and 4)
2. Coal and chalk are relatively soft rocks. Why? (These rocks are found [or formed] on ocean floors and on the earth's surface where there is less pressure, and they are made from organic matter. Rows 2, 3, and 4)
3. Sandstone and shale are harder than chalk and coal. Why? Sandstone and shale are also found on the ocean floor and the earth's surface, but they are made of existing rocks, whereas coal and chalk are made from organic matter. (Rows 2, 3, and 4)

To connect what the students have learned about rocks to other content areas, use such questions as the following:

1. What is Stonehenge? What rocks were used? How was it built? Why does it still last today? (Other examples of interest: the Roman aqueducts, the pyramids)

2. Who are some important sculptors—e.g., Michelangelo—who worked with stone and rock? How did working with rock and stone influence their lives and art?

DISCUSS how useful it is to summarize comparative information on two or more things in a matrix. DISCUSS equivalent uses (see Figure 2c).

Figure 2c. Uses for Matrices in Literature and Content Subjects

---

Comparison	Examples
1. People	Characters in a novel, political leaders, authors
2. Groups	Nations, political groups, cultures, groups within a nation or culture—e.g., minority groups
3. Places	Regions, countries, cities
4. Things	Animals and plants, inanimate objects
5. Time periods	One character or nation at two different time periods, before/after analyses of states or conditions, the stages of development of something
6. Ideas	Ideologies, doctrines, treatises

DISCUSS how to use matrices as mnemonics (memory devices) to study for tests. NOTE that the matrix converts complex information into lists of key words, each of which has rich associations with adjacent words in the matrix and with the column and row headings. (This discussion can lead to a general discussion of how to use graphic outlines to study for tests.)

CONTENT EXAMPLE 3

Content Objective (Literature/Poetry)

Students will read three poems by William Wordsworth—"I Wandered Lonely as a Cloud," "The World Is Too Much with Us," and "My Heart Leaps Up When I Behold"—to understand Wordsworth's perspective about nature and the world, his style, and his use of figurative language.

Overview of Instructional Strategies

Before Focused Instruction: The teacher focuses on understanding poetry as a genre for certain purposes of expression.

During Focused Instruction: The teacher guides students through two of the poems for overall meaning, sensory images, and quality of voice during oral reading.

After Focused Instruction: Students independently practice these processes using the third poem.

BEFORE FOCUSED INSTRUCTION

► *Discuss Objective/Task*

DISCUSS why it is sometimes difficult to understand poetry—e.g., unfamiliar vocabulary and style; use of figurative language.[1]

REVIEW/EXPLAIN the many purposes for reading poetry: to enjoy the rich language, images, and associations; to understand the perspective of the poet; and to understand and use the techniques of the poet.

REVIEW/DISCUSS poetry as a genre that—
1. Uses creative structures.
2. Uses creative language—e.g., figures of speech, symbolism, imagery.
3. Uses oral language patterns—e.g., alliteration.
4. Expresses feelings and thoughts.
5. Recreates experiences, moods, and feelings.
6. Expresses a point of view.[2]

---

[1]**Variation:** DEFINE figurative language and the particular types in Wordsworth's poetry—e.g., simile.
To help students connect figures of speech to their own experience, elicit and discuss figures of speech commonly used in the present time—e.g., "tough as nails," "soft as a kitten."
[2]**Variation:** Assess students' knowlege of these genre characteristics; list them on the chalkboard.

DISCUSS the importance of visualizing sensory images, hearing sound patterns, and evoking word associations while reading poetry.

▶ *Activate Prior Knowlege*

GENERATE characteristics of oral reading and categories for understanding poetry. (See Figure 3a.)

Figure 3a.
Characteristics of Oral Reading and Categories for Understanding Poetry

---

Characteristics of Oral Reading

1. Enunciate words in meaningful idea units (phrasing).
2. Match tempo of voice with rhythm of poem.

Categories for Understanding

1. Recognize richness of language, sensory images evoked, word associations.
2. Identify levels of meaning (literal and interpretive; multiple meanings).
3. Appreciate figurative language—e.g., simile, personification.
4. Reflect on complexity of thought/meaning; experience.
5. Understand the author's perspective about the world.
6. Evaluate the form and genre of the poem as an effective means of communication.

▶ *Provide Information*

EXPLAIN to students that you will read aloud "The World Is Too Much with Us" to model ways to read and interpret poems. Then, students will read orally and interpret the other Wordsworth poems.

DISCUSS the value of rereading something several times for different purposes. READ the poem several times.[3,4,5]

1. For the first reading, THINK ALOUD about the overall meaning, the major theme of the poem. DISCUSS this meaning with the class. (See Figure 3b.)

---

[3]**Variation:** As you read, think aloud ways to figure out meanings for unfamiliar words.
[4]**Variation:** Alternate thinking aloud and asking students to think aloud.
[5]**Variation:** Play recordings of two professional readers reading one of the Wordsworth poems. Ask students to compare the two readings, focusing on the Oral Reading Criteria and the different feelings, reactions, and impressions students have.

Figure 3b. Sample of Thinking Aloud About Overall Meaning

"The World Is Too Much with Us"

The world is too much with us: late and soon,
Getting and spending, we lay waste our powers.
Little we see in nature that is ours;
We have given our hearts away, a sordid boon!
This sea that bares her bosom to the moon,
The winds that will be howling at all hours,
And are gathered up now like sleeping flowers;
For this, for everything, we are out of tune;
It moves us not.—Great God! I'd rather be
A pagan suckled in a creed outworn;
So might I, standing on this pleasant lea,
Have glimpses that would make me less forlorn;
Have sight of Proteus rising from the sea;
Or hear old Triton blow his wreathed horn.

Wordsworth seems to be saying that we have very little connection with nature any more. We pay too much attention to the material world and not enough to the natural world around us. Wordsworth is very critical of that way of living. He would rather live a simpler life and be closer to nature as people used to be. A summary of this poem would be: "People think about the material world too much. They should enjoy, appreciate, and respect nature more than they do."

2. For the second reading, THINK ALOUD how you interpret the figurative language, sensory images, and poet's choice of words: how they evoke specific nuances and contribute to general impressions. Focus especially on how to recognize figures of speech; for example, "This sea that bares her bosom to the moon ..." is an example of personification. The sea does not contain a bosom; a woman does. "The winds ... are gathered up now like sleeping flowers ..." is a simile in which the winds are compared to flowers.

3. For the third reading, FOCUS on quality of voice and characteristics of a good oral reading of poetry. EXPLAIN that much of the enjoyment of poetry comes from hearing the words spoken aloud or hearing one's inner voice speak them (subvocalizing). DISCUSS with students the fact that the oral reading characteristics in Figure 3a may also be criteria for listening to/appreciating poetry.

► *Activate Prior Knowledge*

ASK students if they have ever spent some time watching clouds and wished that they could travel through space as clouds do. ASK students to visualize what a hillside of daffodils might look like if seen from the perspective of a cloud.[6]

---

[6]**Variation:** Ask students to draw pictures of what they think a field of flowers would look like from the point of view of a cloud.

DURING FOCUSED INSTRUCTION

▶ *Construct Meaning for Segments*

ASK a student to read the first stanza of "I Wandered Lonely as a Cloud." GUIDE students to construct the meaning and to interpret the figures of speech about being a cloud and the crowd of daffodils. (See Figure 3c.)

Figure 3c.
Sample of Thinking Aloud About
Overall Meaning and Figures of Speech

Stanza 1: The poet tells how he felt and what he saw as he was walking around the countryside. He compares himself to a cloud: "lonely as a cloud" (simile). In the lines "I saw a crowd, A host of golden daffodils," he uses "crowd" and "host," words we usually associate with groups of human beings, instead of "bunch" or "field of ," words we associate with groups of flowers.

Stanza 2: The poet says that there were flowers everywhere. He compares them to stars: "continuous as the stars that shine"; he says that they "stretched in a never-ending line," that there were "10,000 at a glance" (hyperbole). In the personification "tossing their heads in sprightly dance," he gives the impression that the flowers are happy and free.

Stanza 3: The poet continues the idea that the daffodils are happy: "but they outdid the sparkling waves in glee." He says that seeing the flowers so happy has made him feel happy also. In the last two lines of the stanza, he hints at the important idea developed in the last stanza.

Stanza 4: The poet implies that not only is nature pleasurable at the time people experience it, but also it can remain in memory and keep on giving pleasure just by being recalled.

FOLLOW this procedure for each of the remaining stanzas (see the sample in Figure 3c), scaffolding instruction to allow each reader to take increasing responsibility for constructing meaning.

ENCOURAGE students to evaluate constructively each other's oral readings and interpretations. (See the oral reading characteristics in Figure 3a.)

REREAD or have students reread some of the stanzas for further discussion of word associations, nuances, and sensory images and their contribution to the meaning of the poem.

73

AFTER FOCUSED INSTRUCTION

► *Construct Meaning for the Whole Passage*

DISCUSS the overall meaning of "I Wandered Lonely as a Cloud" (the beauty and comfort of nature and natural form as an end in itself).

► *Extend Learning*

ASK students to use the procedures below to write an interpretation of "My Heart Leaps Up When I Behold." A sample interpretation essay is given below.[7]

1. Review the characteristics of oral reading and categories for understanding poetry in Figure 3a.
2. Read the poem for general impressions and overall meaning.
3. Reread the poem to analyze the meaning of specific lines and figures of speech, taking notes on key points.
4. Use the frame questions for writing about themes in Figure 1b to write an interpretation of the poem.
5. Read the draft three times: first for overall meaning, second for the meaning and style of individual sentences, and third for grammar and punctuation. Revise the draft as needed.
6. Share interpretations with other students.

Sample Essay Interpreting a Poem

"My Heart Leaps Up When I Behold"

Wordsworth feels excitement and joy at seeing a rainbow and, indeed, loves and appreciates everything in nature. He thinks of nature as a unifying force that gives meaning to his life, and he would rather die than live without the excitement of seeing a rainbow. Nature is the important thing that connects and gives meaning to his experiences as a child and as a young man, and that will continue to give meaning in the future when he is an old man.

► *Assess Achievement of Purpose/Learning*

DISCUSS what students have learned about reading and understanding poetry and the meanings of the three Wordsworth poems.

---

[7]**Variation:** Students may work in pairs to write their interpretations.

► *Extend Learning*

WRITE a poem on a topic Wordsworth might have·written about.[8,9]

COMPARE/CONTRAST "I Wandered Lonely as a Cloud" with either of the other two poems. For example, "I Wandered Lonely·as a Cloud" focuses entirely on the joy of nature as an end in itself; in the other two poems, nature is a means of reflecting on life and the world.[10]

Have students LOOK UP *Romanticism* in a dictionary/encyclopedia/literature textbook. DISCUSS the characteristics of Romanticism and how these three poems and/or other poetry by Wordsworth illustrate these characteristics.[11,12]

---

[8]**Variation:** Have students write a class poem.
[9]**Variation:** Have students illustrate or find appropriate photographs from magazines for their poems or the class poem.
[10]**Variation:** Students may record these and other poems by Wordsworth and other Romantic poets to share with the class.
[11]**Variation:** Have students construct a matrix to help them see similarities and differences among literary periods. Cells could contain specific examples of different treatments of nature from representative poems.
[12]**Variation:** Have students compare/constrast one of the Wordsworth poems to the poems of another Romantic poet, or to the poems of a neoclassical or modern poet that deal with nature.

Chapter 5

SKILLS OBJECTIVES

OVERVIEW

There are four broad principles for sequencing skills instruction. The examples in this chapter reflect two of them—but in order to understand these two examples fully, it is useful to explain all four principles.

Four Principles for Sequencing Skills Instruction

The Content-Driven Principle: Using this principle, the teacher selects the skill according to its appropriateness for a given content and task. For example, if the task involves understanding the meaning of specific plays, it is important to comprehend the meaning of each one, to compare them for their similarities in genre, and to contrast these characteristics with some other genre. Thus, a teacher might teach story mapping and/or summarizing as a means of comprehending each play, as well as constructing a matrix for the compare/contrast analysis. This type of instruction, illustrated in Chapter 3, is our strong preference.

One advantage of the content-driven principle of skills instruction is that the skill is selected to help understand the meaning. A disadvantage of this instruction is that students can process only a limited amount of information at once, and the teacher must assess to what extent the skills instruction detracts from learning the content. This is especially true in teaching low-achieving students who often require very explicit skills instruction with scaffolding and ample opportunities to practice the skill and apply it in new contexts. A second disadvantage of this principle is that the teacher may not be able to control the content so that it progresses from easy to difficult. This is particularly important in content courses and basal readers.

The "Lock-Step" Principle: The lock-step principle arises when a school curriculum sequences literally hundreds of discrete skills into a skill hierarchy with little reference to the concepts we have described in this book, such as the use of organizational patterns, scaffolding, increasing complexity, and increasing diversity. Using the lock-step principle, a student may attain mastery in outlining skills by filling in words in a partially completed categorized list in one year; filling in phrases or sentences in a partially completed two-level outline structure in the next year; and filling in phrases or sentences in a partially completed three-level outline structure in the following year—without ever learning to outline complex texts in diverse classroom situations with proficiency.

Thus, the lock-step principle focuses almost exclusively on sequencing skills from easy to difficult without sequencing content toward increasing complexity and increasing diversity in terms of organizational patterns. Nor does there seem to be much effort to vary the degree of teacher support in the lock-step principle. We believe that this "impoverished" concept of skills instruction is the primary reason for much of the criticism of teaching skills objectives as ends in themselves.

The solution to this problem, in our opinion, is not to eliminate adjunct skills courses and separate skills instruction within language arts courses. Instead, our solution to the problem of impoverished skills instruction is to provide "enriched" instruction oriented to the goal of strategic learning. In enriched skills instruction, skills would be taught with reference to specific organizational patterns, with increasing complexity of content, with the coordination of cognitive and metacognitive processes, and with scaffolded instruction leading to student responsibility for learning. In essence, we are suggesting that enriched skills instruction contains many of the elements of cognitive instruction discussed throughout this book. Skills Examples 1 and 2 are intended to reflect enriched skills instruction.

This type of skills instruction has two advantages: (1) the teacher can sequence the content from easy to difficult more easily, and (2) both the teacher and the student can focus on learning the skills, rather than on trying to learn a difficult content and the skills simultaneously. The disadvantage is that it is very difficult to transfer skills from one context to another. However, this problem can be minimized by presenting contrasting organizational patterns with ample opportunities for practice in applying the skill to specific paragraphs and in deciding which organizational pattern is represented.

Enriched Skills Instruction—The Selected Skills Principle: To explain the principle of enriched skills instruction, we refer to the ski analogy cited by several researchers (21, 65). Ultimately, one wants to learn to ski with long skis. However, it is not useful to learn to ski using fragments of the skills needed for skiing with long skis. It would be more productive to learn to ski with short skis, using rudiments of the various skills needed for long skis and increasing the length of the skis as proficiency is gained.

This analogy suggests that, instead of sequencing literally hundreds of discrete subskills from easy to difficult, schools might define a relatively small number of essential skills for each grade level, say 7–20, and focus on teaching them in many different learning contexts. Thus, for the selected skills principle, the easy-to-difficult rule applies to the content and task, not to the skill itself. In this model, the skills selected are critical to thinking and conceptual change, and each one is taught holistically. That is, a complex skill is taught as a whole, and the organizational pattern to which the skill applies is presented as a whole.

Using the selected skills principle, it would be possible to teach even very young students such complex skills as predicting, summarizing, and graphic outlining with ample opportunities to practice the skill with one organizational pattern and then apply it to other patterns. Ideally, this principle should be designed for use with scaffolded instruction, coordination of both cognitive and metacognitive processes, and variations in content and organizational patterns. Skills Example 1 on finding the main idea illustrates the selected skills principle with enriched instruction.

The idea of selecting a few essential skills that are research-based and teaching them throughout the school years is being implemented in schools and states in various ways, and particularly in curriculum guides for the language arts and reading tests in California, Illinois, Michigan, and Wisconsin (see Chapter 3 for discussion and references). Sometimes the implementation is in content courses, and at other times it is in skills courses. Additionally, the Association Collaborative for Teaching Thinking (ACTT), sponsored by the Association for Supervision and Curriculum Development (ASCD), is developing a small list of research-based skills as part of a larger project defining the various dimensions of thinking (69).

Enriched Skills Instruction—The Principle of Clustering Related Skills: This principle of sequencing discrete skills in clusters related to a specific thinking process was referred to in Chapter 1. To recall, M. Pressley, J. G. Borkowski, and W. Schneider (88) indicate that researchers have successfully taught students to combine predicting, finding the main idea, looking for important details, and summarizing in specific learning situations. Thus, while the skills are identifiable in the curriculum as discrete skills, the teacher sequences combinations of them to form a holistic process. In effect, the teacher or curriculum specialist is imposing a more meaningful organization on a given array of skills. This principle also considerably reduces the amount of testing required. In other words, instead of a separate test for each discrete skill, a single test would cover the combined skills and, hopefully, focus more on understanding the content.

This principle of clustering related skills may be useful for teachers who are working with basal series that require the teaching of large numbers of discrete skills. However, using this principle by itself does not mean that the instruction is enriched. For enriched instruction, it is necessary to interweave scaffolding, variances in content and task, and the coordination of cognitive and metacognitive processes. Skills Example 2 on argumentation was devised to illustrate the skills cluster principle. There are some examples of this approach in recent basal readers, adjunct skills programs, and thinking skills programs.

Examples in This Chapter

Skills Example 1 (Finding the Main Idea): Many schools require the teaching of this skill. One reason that finding the main idea is so difficult is that the main idea is often perceived (incorrectly) as "free floating," without reference to the specific paragraph structure in which it is stated or implied (B.B. Armbruster, personal communication).

In reality, many, if not most, of the paragraphs in basals and content texts have main ideas that are embedded, either explicitly or implicitly, in specific organizational patterns such as description or sequence of events. We have even seen the main idea taught in a basal text using a compare/contrast paragraph without any explicit reference to the idea of comparing and contrasting. If students understood that most main ideas are not free floating within a given paragraph and that they may be related to ideas in other paragraphs, finding the main idea and understanding its meaning might be much easier. Yet, finding the main idea (and summarizing, for that matter) is often taught without reference either to the structure of the paragraph(s) or to the process of continually modifying hypotheses about the meaning during and after reading and listening.

Ideally, we should teach finding the main idea using text segments of several paragraphs taken from typical textbooks. However, since most skills instruction involves finding the main idea for unrelated paragraphs, we felt that our instruction should address this reality. Thus, our instruction focuses on teaching the main idea for single paragraphs. Additionally, we use two contrasting organizational patterns to teach the concept that main ideas will vary in their meaning and structure in different organizational patterns.

Skills Example 2 (Argumentation): We selected a cluster of argumentation skills as the second skills example for two reasons. First, there seems to be some confusion about what an argument is; sometimes it is taught indirectly under the guise of opinion paragraphs or other proposition/support paragraphs, rather than focusing on argumentation as a distinct cognitive process in its own right. Second, the skills needed to understand or generate an argument may be fragmented into discrete subskills, such as distinguishing fact and opinion and formulating a generalization, without understanding the structure of an argument as a whole or the criteria for judging it as a whole.

Clearly, an argument consisting of premises and a conclusion *is* a proposition/support paragraph; that is, the conclusion is a proposition and the premises support the conclusion. Thus, simple arguments have the same underlying structure as theme paragraphs and opinion paragraphs. At the same time, arguments are different from other proposition/support paragraphs in two respects. First, at the heart of an argument are the logical relationships among its premises and the conclusion. Second, the criteria for evaluating an argument focus on the relations among the premises and conclusion as well as on the adequacy of the supporting information. Other types of proposition/support paragraphs usually have a somewhat looser structure as well as different criteria for evaluating them, focusing on such issues as whether or not the facts can be verified.

Understanding the structure of an argument is fundamental both to composing them and to comprehending them. Yet argumentation is usually taught only to older students. We believe that it is possible to teach argumentation at many grade levels if it is treated as a holistic process, focusing on whole arguments and varying the materials and complexity of the arguments accordingly. The instruction in Skills Example 2 is an apt beginning to a unit or course on argumentation or critical thinking. That is, our example introduces the skill of identifying premises and conclusions as the first step in a procedure for evaluating arguments. This procedure applies both to arguments to be comprehended and to arguments to be composed. Also, the steps presented in the example's evaluation procedure can serve as pegs for subsequent instruction. How much instruction on argumentation to hang on each peg depends on student abilities and the purpose of the unit or course.

Skills Objective (Finding the Main Idea)

Students will infer the main idea from paragraphs with different types of text structure (grades 4–6).

Overview of Instructional Strategies

This instruction assumes that, generally speaking, main ideas are not "free floating." That is, the content and structure of main idea sentences vary substantially, depending on the purpose and structure or organizational pattern of the paragraph. Thus, this objective requires a great deal of prior knowledge that students often do not acquire from traditional instruction. If the students lack most of the information that we indicate as review, it is useful to teach them the requisite information before this instruction.

Before Focused Instruction: The students review the concept of text structure, signal words for specific text structures, and the process of constructing a main idea.

During Focused Instruction: Small groups of students engage in extensive guided practice in inferring main ideas.

After Focused Instruction: The students discuss what they have learned about inferring main ideas—in particular, when and where it is appropriate to construct different types of main ideas. Students also apply their knowledge of the process to new examples.

BEFORE FOCUSED INSTRUCTION

► *Discuss Objective/Task*

EXPLAIN that inferring the main idea is one skill that strategic readers use to understand and connect ideas. The class will learn how to infer main ideas for two types of paragraphs that are found in content texts.

DISCUSS why it is important to construct main idea statements while reading—e.g, to classify the new information to be learned, to link it to prior knowledge.

► *Activate Prior Knowledge*

EXPLAIN that this lesson will use the K–W–L Strategy Worksheet (76). CONSTRUCT the worksheet in Figure 1a on the chalkboard. (Students should also have their own worksheets at their desks.)

Figure 1a. K–W–L Strategy Worksheet

What We Know	What We Want to Find Out	What We Learn— Still Need to Know

Categories of Information We Expect to Use: Types of Paragraphs

1. Description
2. Problem and solution
3. Compare and contrast
4. Sequence

5. Idea or opinion and support
6. Cause and effect
7. Concept and definition

ELICIT from students what they **know** about main ideas, and LIST this information in the lefthand column on the chalkboard. Students also should **list** this definition on their worksheets.

ASK students what they **want** to learn about finding the main idea. IN- STRUCT them to **list** this information in the middle column of their worksheets.

REVIEW the different types of paragraphs listed at the bottom of the K–W–L Strategy Worksheet.

REVIEW the fact that authors use different organizational patterns or text structures for different purposes and that the main idea sentence will be very different for each type of paragraph.

DISCUSS the purpose of each paragraph listed on the worksheet—e.g., description paragraphs describe persons, places, things, thoughts, and so on; problem/solution paragraphs describe a problem and a solution.

▶ *Focus Interest / Set Specific Purpose*

ASK the students to *select* any two structures—e.g., cause/effect and problem/solution—for focused study.

▶ *Activate Prior Knowledge*

REVIEW the fact that each type of text structure has signal words. ASK the students to *brainstorm* signal words for cause/effect paragraphs and problem/solution paragraphs. LISt these on the chalkboard. (See the appendix at the end of this example for a list of possible signal words.)

DURING FOCUSED INSTRUCTION

EXPLAIN that constructing main ideas is an *interactive thinking process* in which—

1. The reader reads or skims the beginning of a paragraph looking for (a) *clues to the content* and (b) *signal words* for the text structure.

2. The reader then *forms a hypothesis* about the main idea and reads more to refine that hypothesis. To do this, the reader evaluates each new piece of information to see whether or not it supports the hypothesis. If it does not, the hypothesis is modified to accommodate the new information.

EXPLAIN that throughout this process, the reader is *constantly thinking*, selecting important information, rejecting unimportant information, wondering about relationships among ideas, and changing his/her understanding.

EXPLAIN that reading and thinking *are not linear*. The reader does not read line by line from the beginning of the passage to the end. Reading is a start-and-stop process in which the reader reads a bit, thinks a bit, rereads, rethinks, compares new information to what is known, and asks questions.

MODEL this process using a paragraph defining the concept of an animal (see Figure 1b).

Figure 1b. Concept/Definition Paragraph Defining an Animal

Almost everyone can tell an animal from something that is not an animal. How can we tell? We know that an animal is a living thing or an organism. We know that rocks, stars, and houses are not animals because they are not organisms. However, some organisms are not animals. Plants are organisms that are not animals. There are three differences between animals and plants. One difference is that an animal can move voluntarily, or on its own, but a plant cannot. Another difference is that an animal has specialized sense organs, such as eyes and ears, while plants do not. The final difference is that animals cannot make their own food but plants can through the process of photosynthesis.

THINK ALOUD how you figure out the main idea. PROVIDE the following "think aloud" questions in a student worksheet for all students (see Figure 1c).

Figure 1c. Main Idea Frame and Think Aloud Model

Main Idea Frame

Think Aloud Model

1. Skim the passage, pause, and ask yourself;

   a. Are there any words or graphics that signal the text structure?

   b. Are there any graphics or high-lighted words that suggest the content?

   c. Is any information repeated?

   d. What is the passage about?

There are no graphics or words high-lighted with boldfacing, italics, or under-lining. But "animal," "plants," and "dif-ferences" are all repeated. I think this paragraph compares and contrasts plants and animals, but it could be just defining animals, showing how they are different from plants.

2. Begin reading the passage. After the first few sentences, pause and ask yourself:

   a. Do these first few sentences con-firm my hypothesis? If so, do they contain a good main idea sentence?

   b. If not what ideas does my hy-pothesis leave out?

The first few sentences suggest that the paragraph is trying to define what an an-imal is, but I have not found the defini-tion yet. I bet it will be at the end after the differences, if it is given at all.

3. Begin reading again, perhaps to the end of the passage. Then ask yourself:

   a. What is important here?

   b. How can I modify my hypothesis to include all of the important ideas?

The three differences distinguish a plant from an animal. So I guess an animal has special sense organs, moves volun-tarily, and must ingest food.

▶ *Construct Meaning for Segments*

ASK individual students to apply the process to several well-written com-pare/contrast paragraphs. Instruction should be *very scaffolded* here.

1. SELECT a student partner. BEGIN the process of inferring a main idea again, working through the first set of questions in Figure 1b.
2. ASK the class to *evaluate* your reading and thinking, explaining *why* your hypothesis was a good one.

84

3. GUIDE your student partner to *work through* the remaining questions, allowing adequate time for thinking. ASK other students whether or not they accept the reader's interpretation. Encourage students to provide alternate ideas and explanations, where appropriate.
4. FOLLOW these procedures for several new concept/definition paragraphs.

REVIEW the concept of the problem/solution paragraph.

DISCUSS how the main idea statement for such a paragraph will vary from one for a concept/definition paragraph—e.g., the main idea for a problem/solution paragraph will identify the problem(s) and solution(s) in some way.

PROVIDE several problem/solution paragraphs such as the one in Figure 1d. ASK the students to form pairs to *work through* these paragraphs in the same way that they did for the previous set of paragraphs.[1]

Figure 1d. Problem/Solution Paragraph About the Chicago River

---

The Chicago River runs through the heart of the city of Chicago and empties into Lake Michigan. In the 1800s, most of Chicago's waste products were poured into the river. The river carried the waste into Lake Michigan. As Chicagoans dumped millions of gallons of waste into the river, Lake Michigan became increasingly polluted. More and more Chicagoans became sick as a result of drinking the polluted water from Lake Michigan. In fact, many of them died. So Chicago hired engineers to end the pollution, and they decided to keep the waste from flowing into Lake Michigan. They developed a plan to make the Chicago River flow *backwards*. For years, hundreds of men worked to reverse the flow of the river. They completed their work as the new century began. In 1900, the Chicago River no longer flowed into Lake Michigan.

ASK the students to write main idea sentences for several concept/definition paragraphs and problem/solution paragraphs until they have proficiency.

AFTER FOCUSED INSTRUCTION

▶ *Construct Meaning for the Whole Process*

SELECT several students to *review* their understanding of text structures, signal words, and the process of constructing a main idea statement. MAKE CERTAIN that each student fully articulates each idea; ASK other students *to elaborate* if necessary.

---

[1]**Variation:** ASK the students to *write* a think aloud analysis for a short problem/solution paragraph. DIVIDE the class into small groups. DISCUSS the think aloud statements. IDENTIFY and SHARE model statements from each group with the class as a whole.

► *Assess Achievement of Purpose/Learning*

INSTRUCT the students to *write* what they have **learned** and what they still **need to know** on the K–W–L Strategy Worksheet.

► *Extend Learning*

DISCUSS how the class would proceed to infer the main idea for another type of paragraph—e.g., sequential.

DISCUSS the reading/writing relationship—i.e., that the students can use these same concepts about text structures, signal words, and thinking aloud to write paragraphs.

INSTRUCT the class to *construct* a table showing the types of text structures, the signal words for each type, and the purpose of the main idea sentence for each type.

APPENDIX

Signal Words for Different Text Structures

Compare/Contrast

Comparing: like, alike, similarity, similarly, the same as, resemble, have in common, identical, also, share, likewise

Contrasting: in contrast, whereas, instead, different, differences, however, but, although, unlike, then, while, on the one hand, on the other hand, nevertheless, yet

Problem/Solution

Problem: problem, question, puzzle, dissent, disagree, disagreement, limitation, difficulty, need, assessment, the situation, issue, trouble

Solution: solution, answer, respond, response, outcome, result, solve, resolve, satisfy, agree, consent, product, agree, agreement, return, therefore, consequently, thus, wherefore, hence, accordingly

Description

for example, for instance, that is, appears, seems, is, looks like, has/have, is/are, was/were, not, can, does, namely, particularly, specifically, shows, should be/have, could/did, illustrates, typical/typically, characteristic/characteristically, and, additionally/in addition to, moreover, furthermore, further, also, include, besides, another

Sequence

first, second, etc.; before, beforehand, after, afterward, soon, recently, currently, late, later, latter, last/lastly, final/finally, in the end, in the beginning, to start with, to begin with, at the outset, in the final analysis, early, following, as time passed, while, simultaneously, sequentially, at the same time, continuing, years ago, some time ago, foremost, forward, backward, in conclusion, to conclude

Cause/Effect

as a result, because, cause, since, to, in order to, why, purpose, function, if/then, reason, so, in explanation, to explain, therefore, accordingly, thus, hence, led to, in conclusion, to conclude, result, outcome, consequence/consequent product, end, end result, finally, goal

Concept/Example

for example, exemplar, a case in point, for instance, relation, relationship, concept, conceptually, set, subset, subordinate, superordinate, category, connection

Proposition/Support

reason, reason for, opinion, opine, think, reason, argue, in support of, counterargument, countered, contended, maintained, suggests, indicate, demonstrate, show, illustrate, put forth/forward, propose, proposition, suppose, presuppose, premise, assume, presume, pretend, hypothesize, hypothetical, formulate, articulate, enumerate, charge, portend, witness, appears, seems, seemingly, evidently, apparently, if/then, proof

Skills Objective (Argumentation)

Students will identify the premises and conclusion of an argument (grade 7–high school).

Overview of Instructional Strategies

The instruction presented is most appropriate for high school students. However, Lipman's *Philosophy for Children* program (98) strongly suggests that even younger children can learn about argumentation. Modifications such as slowing the pace, using more examples, and supplying more scaffolding can help make this instruction more appropriate for middle school students.

This instruction introduces students to the first step in a procedure for analyzing arguments. Each step in the procedure can serve as the basis for a large block of instruction. In fact, the procedure could serve as the cornerstone of a critical thinking course.

Before Focused Instruction: The teacher leads a discussion of arguments and their value, introduces new vocabulary, and elicits hypotheses about how to identify an argument's premises and conclusion.

During Focused Instruction: Student pairs identify premises and conclusions in arguments after the teacher models the process.

After Focused Instruction: The students discuss the process and diffficulties in carrying it out. Individual students then find arguments in the real world and identify premises and conclusions. Students have opportunities to apply their knowledge of the process of identifying premises and conclusions while writing vignettes and studying advertisements.

BEFORE FOCUSED INSTRUCTION

▶ *Discuss Objective/Task*

Ask students to examine Figure 2a and EXPLAIN that students will learn a procedure for analyzing arguments. Arguments have two parts: the premises and the conclusion. Analyzing an argument consists of identifying these parts and then evaluating the relations among them. This instruction focuses on identifying the parts of an argument.

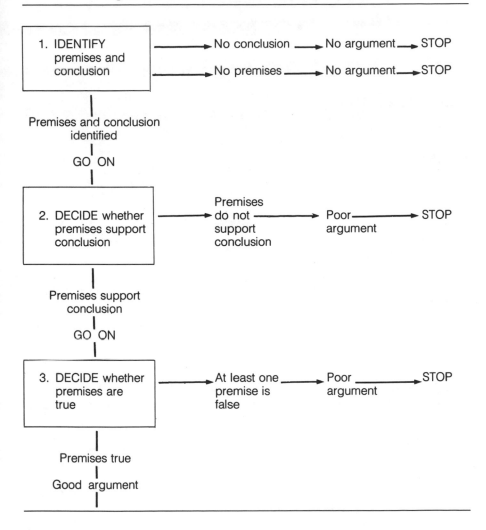

Figure 2a. The Process for Analyzing Arguments

1. IDENTIFY premises and conclusion
→ No conclusion → No argument → STOP
→ No premises → No argument → STOP

Premises and conclusion identified
GO ON

2. DECIDE whether premises support conclusion
→ Premises do not support conclusion → Poor argument → STOP

Premises support conclusion
GO ON

3. DECIDE whether premises are true
→ At least one premise is false → Poor argument → STOP

Premises true

Good argument

► *Activate Prior Knowledge*

ELICIT definitions of an argument, a premise, and a conclusion. For example:

- *argument*: a belief or an action and its support; two people yelling at each other
- *premise*: a reason for believing or acting; support for one's position
- *conclusion*: an opinion that you can support; a reasonable belief or action

89

ASK students to study the vocabulary and examples in Figure 2b.

Figure 2b. Argument Vocabulary and Examples

---

argument: an opinion or action and the reasons for having the opinion or performing the action

premise: a reason for having an opinion or for performing an action

conclusion: the opinion or action for which reasons are given

Examples: A		B
1. If humans always act from self-interest, then acting morally is impossible.	PREMISE	1. Killing an animal causes the animal pain.
2. Acting morally is possible.	PREMISE	2. We should not cause animals pain.
3. Humans do not always act from self-interest.	CONCLUSION	3. We should not kill animals.

DISCUSS similarities and differences among student definitions and the definitions in Figure 2b.

ELICIT which argument concludes with an action (B in Figure 2b) and which concludes with an opinion (A in Figure 2b). Elicit *simple* examples of each kind.

▶ *Focus Interest / Set Specific Purpose*

DISCUSS where one hears and reads arguments. Arguments are found almost everywhere—e.g., in the editorial pages of newspapers, in parent/child discussions of what the child should do, in court.

DISCUSS why it is valuable to analyze (identify and evaluate) arguments—e.g., so one will act from good reasons; so one will not be fooled. If necessary, GIVE an example in which one is fooled or does not act from good reasons, such as buying a particular kind of jeans because an advertisement says wearing them will make one popular.

EXPLAIN that an argument is a way of organizing or structuring information. The conclusion of an argument is like the main idea of a paragraph. The premises are like the supporting details. The structure of a simple argument is the same as that for a *proposition/support* paragraph. An argument is distinguished from other proposition/support paragraphs by the focus on understanding the logic among the sentences and by the idea that arguments can be evaluated as being good or bad, based on the logic and the adequacy of the information.

ELICIT hypotheses about how one might identify the premises and conclusion of an argument—e.g., signal words, relations among sentences, questions like "Does this sentence support another or is it supported by another?"

DURING FOCUSED INSTRUCTION

EXPLAIN that you will model how to identify the premises and conclusion of an argument. (Students should have a written copy of the argument.)

ASK students to compare your model with their hypotheses about identifying the premises and conclusion of an argument. (See Figure 2c for an example of modeling.)

▶ *Clarify Ideas*

ELICIT the observation that some sentences in the letter were not parts of the argument and that you used signal words and connections among sentences to identify the premises and the conclusion of the argument. In short, the organization of the letter and the signals of its organization were what you used to identify the parts of the argument.

ASK students to brainstorm signal words for premises and conclusions. The most reliable are as follows:
* *conclusion*: therefore, hence, in conclusion, so, thus, consequently, it follows that, this implies
* *premise*: for, because, if, since, the reason is.

Less reliable signal words are listed under *proposition/support* in the appendix to Skills Example 1.

▶ *Construct Meaning for Segments*

ASK pairs of students to identify the premises and conclusions in two arguments. One should do the identification while "talking through" the process. The other should monitor the identifier's progress, make suggestions, point out problems, etc. Students switch roles after completing their work on one argument.

ELICIT from students the premises and conclusions of the two arguments and map the structure of the arguments on the chalkboard.

Figure 2c.
An Example of Thinking Aloud to Identify
the Premises and Conclusion in an Argument

Argument	Model
1. To the editor:	This argument seems to come from a newspaper or magazine.
2. The school board has done it again.	This sentence does not tell me much. I cannot even tell whether the writer likes or dislikes what the school board has done. I need to read more to find out the purpose of this sentence.
3. Last Tuesday night, it allocated 25 percent more funds to men's sports than to women's sports.	This seems to be what the board has done again. However, I cannot tell whether this sentence begins the argument or not. Maybe this sentence and the first sentence are just stage setting. I'll move on.
4. The board's action is unconstitutional.	This suggests that the writer disagrees with the school board. Maybe this is what the writer will argue for.
5. Everyone knows that the Constitution guarantees equal opportunity for all U.S. citizens.	This sounds like part of the reason why the board's action is unconstitutional. If it is, then this sentence is a premise and the previous sentence is the conclusion.
6. More funds for men's sports provides more opportunities for men than for women.	This sentence links the premise and the conclusion I just identified. So I think this sentence is another premise.
7. Therefore, the board's allocation of funds to men's and *women's sports is unconstitu-*tional.	This sentence restates what I thought was the conclusion. It also starts with the word *therefore,* which indicates that what comes before supports what comes after. So I think I've correctly identified the conclusion and the premises.
8. I urge the board to reconsider its action.	The argument seems to be finished. This sentence is not a reason for the conclusion that the board's action is unconstitutional. Rather, it is a call for action based on the argument.
9. Sincerely, Lou Smith	

AFTER FOCUSED INSTRUCTION

▶ *Construct Meaning for the Whole Process*

ELICIT descriptions of the thinking processes students used to identify the premises and conclusions in the arguments, in particular when there were few signal words in the argument. For example, they might have looked for support relations among sentences or crossed out sentences that were not part of the argument.

▶ *Assess Achievement of Purpose/Learning*

REVIEW what was learned: the definitions of an argument, premises, and conclusions, and the procedures for identifying the structure of an argument.

▶ *Extend Learning*

INSTRUCT the students to find in a periodical a short editorial or letter-to-the-editor containing an argument and then to identify and record the premises and conclusion of the argument. (Students can use these editorials or letters when they learn about evaluating arguments.)

ASK students to do one of the following:
- Write a brief essay presenting students' arguments for coming to school today or for going to college.
- Write a vignette about someone arguing with him/herself about an important decision or a moral action.
- Think of an advertisment as an argument, and then pick an advertisement and identify its premises and conclusion.

These various compositions consolidate previous learning and provide bridges to new learning.

GLOSSARY

The terms in this glossary have acquired special meanings in current educational research. We have provided these meanings because special nuances of the terms may not have been well communicated to teachers.

activation: the "calling up" of appropriate knowledge structures (or schema), of strategies and/or content, for use in a learning task; the process may be largely unconscious and usually involves making inferences.

articulation: the verbalization of specific knowledge, reasoning, or problem-solving processes (25).

clarification: the identification and resolution of problems one has in understanding a text—e.g., contradictions or inconsistencies (25).

coaching: the diagnosis and correction of a student's approach to a task; may be part of scaffolded instruction; may involve modeling (25).

cognitive instruction: instructional strategies and approaches that facilitate higher-level thinking and independent learning.

comprehension/construction of meaning: goal-oriented, active processing to derive meaning from a text (reading/listening) or to create meaning in a text (writing/speaking); depends at least in part on the purpose of the task and prior knowledge.

content-driven skills instruction: the content to be taught determines which skills will be taught as opposed to sequencing skills from easy to difficult and selecting content to teach those skills.

direct instruction 1 (cognitive psychology perspective): an approach to teaching strategies that explicitly informs students as to the nature of a strategy, how it works, why it should be used, and where and when to use it (84).

direct instruction 2 (research on teaching perspective): a sequence of teaching functions including review of just completed work and homework, presentation, guided practice, feedback and correctives, and review of weekly and monthly work.

domain knowledge: the conceptual knowledge and procedures associated with a particular content area (25).

fading: the gradual shift of responsibility for accomplishing a learning task from teacher to students (25).

frame: a set of questions or categories of information implied by a particular text structure; *content frames* pertain to specific content areas; *generic frames* can be used across content areas (see Planning Guide 2).

94

graphic mapping: the process of transforming linear text into nonlinear patterns—e.g., compare/contrast matrices, flowcharts.

heuristics: a series of thinking steps/rules of thumb for accomplishing a task; may or may not be content-specific (25).

informed strategic learning (ISL): acquiring metacognitive strategies through explicit instruction (84).

instructional episode/cycle: a sequence of instruction that has three phases—before, during, and after; has a focal point/purpose—e.g., a particular content or process; is highly recursive (see *learning episode/cycle*).

knowledge structure: the sum of what a student knows about a given content or strategy; the systematic organization of knowledge and thinking (see *schema*).

learning episode/cycle: a sequence of learning that has three phases—before, during, and after; has a focal point/purpose—e.g., a particular content or process; is highly recursive (see *instructional episode/cycle*).

learning strategies: a systematic plan for learning new content or new plans (strategies).

mediation: an instructional approach in which the teacher intercedes between students and instructional materials/learning problem in order to help students construct meaning, especially higher-level meaning.

metacognition: a student's conscious attention to and control of his/her process/progress in a learning task; thinking about one's own learning.

modeling: an instructional strategy in which the teacher demonstrates how to do a task.

monitoring strategies: the systematic plans for a particular learning task; monitoring strategies have both a diagnostic and a remedial component (25).

prior knowledge: the sum of a student's knowledge gained from previous experiences in and out of school.

reading across the curriculum (RAC): a philosophy that all teachers should deal with comprehension plus a cluster of strategies for learning in content areas (50).

reciprocal teaching: instruction in which teachers and students alternate taking the teacher role with students gradually assuming full responsibility (81).

response instruction: providing explicit information about how to respond to questions, especially written responses; provides information about both product and process (58).

scaffolding instruction: providing teacher support to students by modeling the thought processes in a learning episode and gradually shifting the responsibility of formulating questions and thinking aloud to students themselves.

schema: a generalized description, plan, or structure; a conceptual system for understanding something (see *knowledge structure*).

signal words: the words or phrases that indicate a text structure—e.g., "first," "second," etc., for a sequential text structure.

skill: an acquired ability to perform well—e.g., determining the main idea of a paragraph (see *strategy*).

strategic learning: a concept of learning that recognizes that students have a repertoire of learning strategies to apply in learning tasks (see Planning Guide 1) (85).

strategic teaching: an approach to teaching that recognizes that teachers have a repertoire of instructional strategies to apply in instructional episodes (see Planning Guide 3).

strategy: a systematic plan for achieving a specific goal or result—e.g., predicting (48).

text: any potentially meaningful message that occurs in print, graphics, speech, or other media.

text structures: specific organizational patterns such as compare/contrast, cause/effect, and description.

BIBLIOGRAPHY

1. Alverman, D. E. "The Compensatory Effect of Graphic Organizers on Descriptive Text." *Journal of Educational Research* 75 (1981): 44–48.

2. _____. "Restructuring Text Facilitates Written Recall of Main Ideas." *Journal of Reading* 25 (1982): 754–58.

3. Anderson, C. W., and Smith, L. "Teaching Science." In *The Educator's Handbook: A Research Perspective*, edited by V. Koehler. In press.

4. Anderson, R. C. "Role of Reader's Schema in Comprehension, Learning, and Memory." In *Learning to Read in American Schools: Basal Readers and Content Texts*, edited by R. C. Anderson, J. Osborn, and R. J. Tierney. Hillsdale, N.J.: Erlbaum, 1984. pp. 243–59.

5. _____, and others. *Becoming a Nation of Readers: The Report of the Commission on Reading*. Urbana: University of Illinois, 1985.

6. Anderson, T. H. "Study Strategies and Adjunct Aids." In *Cognitive and Affective Learning Strategies*, edited by R. Spiro, B.C. Bruce, and W. F. Brewer. Hillsdale, N.J.: Erlbaum, 1980. pp. 483–502.

7. _____, and Armbruster, B. B. "Content Area Textbooks." In *Learning to Read in American Schools: Basal Readers and Content Texts*, edited by R. C. Anderson, J. Osborn, and R.J. Tierney. Hillsdale, N.J.: Erlbaum, 1984. pp. 193–226.

8. _____, "Studying." In *Handbook of Reading Research*, edited by P. D. Pearson. New York: Longman, 1985. pp. 657–80.

9. Applebee, A. N. "Writing and Reasoning." *Review of Educational Research* 54 (1984): 577–96.

10. Armbruster, B. B. "Schema Theory and the Design of Instructional Text." *Educational Psychologist*. In press.

11. _____, and Anderson, T. H. "Frames: Structure for Informational Texts." In *Technology of Text*, edited by D. H. Jonassen. Vol. 2. Englewood Cliffs, N.J.: Educational Technology Publications, 1985. pp. 90–104.

12. Bean, T. W.; Singer, H.; and Cowen, S. "Acquisition of a Topic Schema in High School Biology Through an Onological Study Guide." In *Issues in Literacy: A Research Perspective*, edited by J. A. Niles and R. V. Lalik. Thirty-Fourth Yearbook of the National Reading Conference. Rochester, N.Y.: National Reading Conference, 1985. pp. 38–42.

13. _____, and others. "The Effect of Metacognition Instruction in Outlining and Graphic Organizer Construction on Students' Comprehension in a Tenth-Grade World History Class." *Journal of Reading Behavior* 18 (1986): 153–70.

14. Beck, I. L.; Perfetti, C. A.; and McKeown, M. C. "The Effects of Long-Term Vocabulary Instruction on Lexical Access and Reading Comprehension." *Journal of Educational Psychology* 74 (1982): 506–21.

15. Berliner, D. C. "The Executive Functions of Teaching." Paper presented at the Wingspread conference relating reading research to classroom instruction, Wingspread, Racine, Wisconsin, and at the annual meeting of the American Educational Research Association, New York, March 1982.

16. _____. "The Half-Full Glass: A Review of Research in Teaching." In *Using What We Know About Teaching*, edited by P. L. Hosford. Alexandria, Va.: Association for Supervision and Curriculum Development, 1984. pp. 51–77.

17. _____. "In Pursuit of the Expert Pedagogue." Presidential address presented at the annual meeting of the American Educational Research Association, San Francisco, April 1986.

18. Brown, A. L. *Teaching Students to Think as They Read: Implications for Curriculum Reform*. Reading Education Report No. 58. Urbana: University of Illinois, The Center for the Study of Reading, 1985.

19. _____; Armbruster, B. B.; and Baker, L. "The Role of Metacognition and Studying." In *Reading Comprehension: From Research to Practice*, edited by J. Orasanu. Hillsdale, N.J.: Erlbaum, 1985.

20. _____, and others. "Learning, Remembering, and Understanding." In *Handbook of Child Psychology*, edited by J. H. Flavell and E. M. Markham. Vol. 3. New York: John Wiley, 1983. pp. 77–166.

21. Burton, R.; Brown, J. S.; and Fischer, G. "Skiing as a Model of Instruction." In *Everyday Cognition: Its Development in Social Context*, edited by B. Rogoff and J. Lave. Cambridge, Mass.: Harvard University Press, 1984. pp. 139–50.

22. California State Board of Education. "English/Language Arts." In *Model Curriculum Standards: Grades Nine Through Twelve*. Sacramento: California State Department of Education, 1985.

23. Carr, E. "Vocabulary Overview Guide." In *Teaching Reading as Thinking*, edited by A. S. Palincsar and others. Facilitator's Manual. Alexandria, Va.: Association for Supervision and Curriculum Development, 1986. pp. 1–5.

24. Chance P. *Thinking in the Classroom*. New York: Teacher's College Press, 1986. pp. 101–107.

25. Collins, A., and Brown, J. S. "Cognitive Apprenticeship: Teaching Students the Craft of Reading, Writing, and Mathematics." In *Cognition and Instruction: Issues and Agendas*, edited by L. B. Resnick. In press.

26. _____; Brown, J. S.; and Larkin, K. M. "Inference in Text Understanding." In *Theoretical Issues in Reading Comprehension*, edited by R. J. Spiro, B. C. Bruce, and W. F. Brewer. Hillsdale, N.J.: Erlbaum, 1980. pp. 385–410.

27. Cooper, C. R., and Matsuhashi, A. "A Theory of the Writing Process." In *The Psychology of Written Language*. New York: John Wiley, 1983.

28. Dansereau, D. F. "Learning Strategy Research." In *Thinking and Learning Skills: Relating Instruction to Research*, edited by J. W. Segal, S. F.

98

Chipman, and R. Glaser. Vol. 1. Hillsdale, N.J.: Erlbaum, 1985. pp. 209–40.

29. Davey, B. "Think Aloud—Modeling the Cognitive Processes of Reading Comprehension." *Journal of Reading* (1983): 44–47.

30. Delia, J. G. "Constructivism and the Study of Human Communication." *Quarterly Journal of Speech* 63 (1977): 66–89.

31. Derry, S. J., and Murphy, D. A. "Designing Systems That Train Learning Ability: From Theory to Practice." *Review of Educational Research* 56 (1986): 1–39.

32. Devine, T. G. *Listening Skills Schoolwide: Activities and Programs*. Urbana, Ill.: National Council of Teachers of English, 1982.

33. Duchastel, P. C. "Textual Display Techniques." In *Principles for Structuring, Designing, and Displaying Text*, edited by D. Jonassen. Englewood Cliffs, N.J.: Educational Technology Publications, 1982.

34. Duckwork, K., and Bevoise, W. D. *Student Engagement and Skill Development in Writing at the Secondary Level*. Technical Report. Eugene, Oreg.: Center for Educational Policy and Management, 1986.

35. Duffy, G. G.; Roehler, L. R.; and Rackliffe, G. "Student Cognitive Processing of Teacher Explanations During Reading Instruction." Paper presented at the annual meeting of the American Educational Research Association, Chicago, April 1985.

36. Durkin, D. "What Classroom Observations Reveal About Reading Comprehension Instruction." *Reading Research Quarterly* 4 (1978–79): 515–44.

37. Feuerstein, R. *Instrumental Enrichment*. Baltimore: University Park Press, 1980.

38. _____, and Jensen, M. R. "Instrumental Enrichment: Theoretical Basis, Goals, and Instruments." *The Educational Forum* 46 (1980): 401–23.

39. Fisher, C., and others. *Teaching and Learning in Elementary Schools: A Summary of the Beginning Teacher Evaluation Study*. San Francisco: Far West Laboratory, 1978.

40. Flower, L., and Hayes, J. R. "The Pregnant Pause: An Enquiry into the Nature of Planning." *Research in the Teaching of English* 15 (1981): 229–44.

41. Friedman, L. B., and Tinzmann, M. "Graphics in Middle-Grade U.S. History Textbooks." In *Issues in Literacy: A Research Perspective*, edited by J. Niles and R. Lalik. Thirty-Fourth Yearbook of the National Reading Conference. Rochester, N.Y.: National Reading Conference, 1985.

42. Friedman, P. *Listening Processes: Attention, Understanding, Evaluation*. 2d ed. Washington, D.C.: National Education Association, 1986.

43. Garner, R., and others. "Inducing Use of a Text Lookback Strategy Among Unsuccessful Readers." *American Educational Research Journal* 21 (1984): 789–98.

44. Gersten, R., and Carnine, D. "Direct Instruction in Reading Comprehen-

sion." *Educational Leadership* 43 (1986): 70–78.

45. Good, T. L., and Brophy, J. E. *Looking in Classrooms*. Cambridge, Mass.: Harper & Row, 1984.

46. Graves, D. H. *Balance the Basics: Let Them Write*. New York: The Ford Foundation, 1978.

47. Hale, C. L. "A Constructivist Approach to Meaning: In Defense of Interpretation." In *Argument and Social Practice: Proceedings of the Fourth SCA/AFA Conference on Argumentation*, edited by J. R. Cox, M. O. Sillars, and G. B. Walker. Washington, D.C.: Speech Communication Association, 1985. pp. 523–34.

48. Harris, T. L., and Hodges, R. E., eds. *Dictionary of Reading and Related Terms*. Newark, Del.: International Reading Association, 1981.

49. Herber, H. L. "Developing Reading and Thinking Skills in Content Areas." In *Thinking and Learning Skills: Relating Instruction to Research*, edited by J. W. Segal, S. F. Chipman, and R. Glaser. Vol. 1. Hillsdale, N.J.: Erlbaum, 1985. pp. 297–316.

50. _____. *Reading in the Content Areas*. Englewood Cliffs, N.J.: Prentice-Hall, 1978.

51. Idol-Maestas, L., and Croll, V. J. *The Effects of Training in Story Mapping Procedures on the Reading Comprehension of Poor Readers*. Technical Report No. 352. Urbana: University of Illinois, The Center for the Study of Reading, 1986.

52. Johnson, D. D., and Pearson, P. D. *Teaching Vocabulary Comprehension*. New York: Holt, Rinehart & Winston, 1984.

53. _____; Pittelman, S. D.; and Heimlich, J. E. "Semantic Mapping." *The Reading Teacher* 39 (1986): 778–83.

54. Jonassen, D. H. "Generative Learning vs. Mathemagenic Control of Text Processing." In *The Technology of Text*, edited by D. H. Jonassen. Vol. 2. Englewood Cliffs, N.J.: Educational Technology Press, 1985. pp. 9–45.

55. _____. " Patterns for Mapping Cognitive Structure." Paper presented at the annual convention of the Association for Educational Communication and Technology, New Orleans, 1983.

56. Jones, B. F. "Reading and Thinking." In *Developing Minds: A Resource Book for Teaching Thinking*, edited by A. Costa. Alexandria, Va.: Association for Supervision and Curriculum Development, 1985. pp. 108–13.

57. _____. "Research-Based Guidelines for Constructing Graphic Representations of Text." Paper presented at the annual meeting of the American Educational Research Association, Chicago, April 1985.

58. _____. "Response Instruction." In *Reading, Thinking, and Conceptual Development: Strategies for the Classroom*, edited by T. L. Harris and E. J. Cooper. New York: The College Board, 1985. pp. 105–28.

59. _____. "SPaRCS Procedure." In *Teaching Reading as Thinking*, edited by A. S. Palincsar and others. Facilitator's Manual. Alexandria, Va.: Association for Supervision and Curriculum Development, 1986. pp. 11–18.

60. _____.; Amiran, M. R.; and Katims, M. "Teaching Cognitive Strategies and Text Structures Within Language Arts Programs." In *Thinking and Learning Skills: Relating Instruction to Research*, edited by J. W. Segal, S. F. Chipman, and R. Glaser. Vol. 1. Hillsdale, N.J.: Erlbaum, 1985. pp. 259-96.

61. _____, and others. *Content-Driven Comprehension Instruction: A Model for Army Training Literature*. Technical Report. Alexandria, Va.: Army Research Institute, 1984.

62. _____, and others, eds. *A Framework for Cognitive Instruction and Applications to the Content Areas*. In preparation.

63. LaFleur, G. D. "A New Look at Meaning in Systems to Argument." In *Argument and Social Practice: Proceedings of the Fourth SCA/AFA Conference on Argumentation*, edited by J. R. Cox, M. O. Sillars, and G. B. Walker. Washington, D.C.: Speech Communication Association, 1985.

64. Leinhardt, G. "Expertise in Mathematics Teaching." *Educational Leadership* 43 (1986): 23-27.

65. Lesgold, A. M. "Producing Automatic Performance." Paper presented at the annual meeting of the American Educational Research Association, San Francisco, April 1986.

66. Lundsteen, S. W. *Listening: Its Impact at All Levels on Reading and the Other Language Arts*. Urbana, Ill.: National Council of Teachers of English, 1979.

67. Lunzer, E.; Davies, F.; and Green, T. *Reading for Learning in Science*. School Council Project Report. Nottingham, England: University of Nottingham, School of Education, 1980.

68. Markle, S. M. "They Teach Concepts, Don't They?" *Educational Researcher* 4 (1975): 3-9.

69. Marzano, R., and others. *Dimensions of Thinking*. Alexandria, Va.: Association for Supervision and Curriculum Development, forthcoming.

70. Mayer, R. E. "Aids to Text Comprehension." *Educational Psychologist* 19 (1984): 30-42.

71. McCutchen, D. "Domain Knowledge and Linguistic Knowledge in the Development of Writing Ability." *Journal of Memory and Language*. In press.

72. Meyer, B. J. F. "Reading Research and the Composition Teacher: The Importance of Plans." *College Composition and Communication* 33 (1982): 37-49.

73. _____; Brandt, D. M.; and Bluth, G. C. "Use of Top-Level Structure in Text: Key for Reading Comprehension of Ninth-Grade Students." *Reading Research Quarterly* 16 (1980): 72-103.

74. _____, and Freedle, R. O. "Effects of Discourse Type on Recall." *American Educational Research Journal* 21 (1984): 121-43.

75. Mezynski, K. "Issues Concerning the Acquisition of Knowledge: Effects of Vocabulary Training on Reading Comprehension." *Review of Educational*

Research 53 (1983): 253–79.

76. Michigan Reading Association and Michigan Department of Education. *What Research Says to the Classroom Teacher About Reading*. Lansing: Communications/MEAP Ad Hoc Committee and the Michigan Reading Association, 1985.

77. Nagy, W. E., and Herman, P. A. "Incidental Instructional Approaches to Increase Reading Vocabulary." *Educational Perspectives* 23 (1985): 16–21.

78. Ogle, D. S. "K–W–L: A Teaching Model That Develops Active Reading of Expository Text." *The Reading Teacher* 39 (1986): 564–71.

79. Orange County Public Schools. *Reading in the Content Area (RICA)*. Orlando, Fla.: Orange County Public Schools, 1985.

80. Palincsar, A. S. "The Role of Dialogue in Providing Scaffolded Instruction." *Educational Psychologist* 21 (1986): 73–98.

81. _____, and Brown, A. L. "Reciprocal Teaching: Activities to Promote 'Reading with Your Mind.'" In *Reading, Thinking, and Concept Development: Strategies for the Classroom*, edited by T. L. Harris and E. J. Cooper. New York: The College Board, 1985. pp. 147–60.

82. _____, and others, eds. *Teaching Reading as Thinking*. Facilitator's Manual. Alexandria, Va.: Association for Supervision and Curriculum Development, 1986.

83. Paris, P.; Scardamalia, M.; and Bereiter, C. "Discourse Schemata as Knowledge and as Regulators of Text Production." Paper presented at the annual meeting of the American Educational Research Association, Boston, April 1980.

84. Paris, S. G.; Cross, D. R.; and Lipson, M. Y. "Informed Strategies for Learning: A Program to Improve Children's Reading Awareness and Comprehension." *Journal of Educational Psychology* 76 (1984): 1239–52.

85. _____; Lipson, M. Y.; and Wixson, K. "Becoming a Strategic Reader." *Contemporary Educational Psychology* 8 (1983): 293–316.

86. Pearson, P. D., and Gallagher, M. C. "The Instruction of Reading Comprehension." *Contemporary Educational Psychology* 8 (1983): 317–44.

87. _____, and Tierney, R. J. "On Becoming a Thoughtful Reader: Learning to Read Like a Writer." In *Yearbook of the National Society for the Study of Education*. Vol. 83, Part 1, *Becoming Readers in a Complex Society*. Chicago: National Society for the Study of Education, 1984. pp. 144–73.

88. Pressley, M.; Borkowski, J. G.; and Schneider, W. "Good Strategy Users Coordinate Metacognition, Strategy Use and Knowledge." In *Annals of Child Development*, edited by R. Vasta and G. Whitehurst. In press.

89. Raphael, T. E., and Kirschner, B. M. *The Effects of Instruction in Compare/Contrast Text Structure on Sixth-Grade Students' Reading Comprehension and Writing Products*. Research Series 161. East Lansing: Michigan State University, Institute for Research on Teaching, 1985.

90. Resnick, L. B. *Education and Learning to Think*. Special report prepared for the Commission on Behavioral and Social Sciences and Education,

National Research Council. 1985.

91. Rosenshine, B. V. "Synthesis of Research on Explicit Teaching." *Educational Leadership* 43 (1986): 60–69.

92. _____. "Teaching Functions in Instructional Programs." *The Elementary School Journal* 83 (1983): 335–51.

93. Roth, K. J. "Conceptual Change, Learning, and Student Processing of Science Texts." Paper presented at the annual meeting of the American Educational Research Association, San Francisco, 1985.

94. Scardamalia, M., and Bereiter, C. "Research on Written Composition." In *Handbook of Research on Teaching*, edited by M. C. Wittrock. 3d ed. New York: Macmillan, 1985. pp. 59–84.

95. _____. "Teachability of Reflective Processes in Written Composition." *Cognitive Science* 8 (1984): 173–90.

96. Schallert, D. L.; Alexander, P. A.; and Goetz, E. T. "What Do Instructors and Authors Do to Influence the Textbook-Student Relationship?" In *Issues in Literacy: A Research Perspective*, edited by J. A. Niles and R. V. Lalik. Thirty-Fourth Yearbook of The National Reading Conference. Rochester, N.Y.: National Reading Conference, 1985.

97. Shimmerlik, S. M. "Organization Theory and Memory for Prose: A Review of the Literature." *Review of Educational Research* 48 (1978): 103–21.

98. Shipman, V. C. "Evaluation Replication of the Philosophy for Children Program (Final Report)." *Thinking* 5 (1983): 45–47.

99. Singer, H., and Bean, T. *Relationship Between Ability to Learn from Text and Achievement in the UC and CSU Systems*. Technical Report No. 3. Learning from Text Project, Executive Summary. 1983.

100. _____, and Donlan, D. "Active Comprehension: Problem-Solving Schema with Question Generation for Comprehension of Complex Short Stories." *Reading Research Quarterly* 17 (1982): 166–86.

101. Spiro, R. J., and Myers, A. "Individual Differences and Underlying Cognitive Processes in Reading." In *Handbook of Reading Research*, edited by P. D. Pearson. New York: Longman, 1984. pp. 471–501.

102. Stein, N. L., and Glenn, C. G. "An Analysis of Story Comprehension in Elementary School Children." In *New Directions in Discourse Processing*, edited by R. Freedle. Norwood, N.J.: Ablex, 1979.

103. Stubbs, M. *Language and Literacy: The Sociolinguistics of Reading and Writing*. London: Routledge & Kegan Paul, 1980.

104. Taylor, B. M. "Text Structure and Children's Comprehension and Memory for Expository Material." *Journal of Educational Psychology* 74 (1982): 323–40.

105. Tierney, R. J. *Learning From Text*. Reading Education Report No. 37. Urbana: University of Illinois, The Center for the Study of Reading, 1983.

106. _____; Readence, J. E.; and Dishner, E. K. *Reading Strategies and Practices—A Compendium*. 2d ed. Boston: Allyn & Bacon, 1985.

107. Toulmin, S.; Janik, A.; and Rieke, R. *An Introduction to Reasoning*. New York: Macmillan, 1984.

108. Weinstein, C. E., and Mayer, R. E. "The Teaching of Learning Strategies." In *Handbook of Research on Teaching*, edited by M. C. Wittrock. 3d ed. New York: Macmillan, 1985.

109. _____, and Underwood, V. L. "Learning Strategies: The *How* of Learning." In *Thinking and Learning Skills: Relating Instruction to Research*, edited by J. W. Segal, S. F. Chipman, and R. Glaser. Vol. 1. Hillsdale, N.J.: Erlbaum, 1985. pp. 241–58.

110. Winne, P., and Marx, R. W. *Student Cognitive Processes While Learning from Teaching*. Vols. 1 and 2. Instructional Psychology Research Group (NIE Final Report, Grant No. NIE–G–79–0098). Burnaby, British Columbia: Simon Frasier University, 1983.

111. Wisconsin Department of Public Instruction. *A Guide to Curriculum Planning in Reading*, edited by D. Cook. Madison: Wisconsin Department of Public Instruction, 1986.

112. Wittrock, M. C. *Generative Reading Comprehension*. Ginn Occasional Reports. Boston: Ginn, 1983.

113. _____. "Students' Thought Processes." In *Handbook of Research on Teaching*, edited by M. C. Wittrock. 3d ed. New York: Macmillan, 1985.

114. Wolvin, A. D., and Coakley, C. G. *Listening Instruction* (A theory and research monograph). Urbana, Ill.: ERIC Clearinghouse on Reading and Communication Skills; Annandale, Va.: Speech Communication Association, 1975.